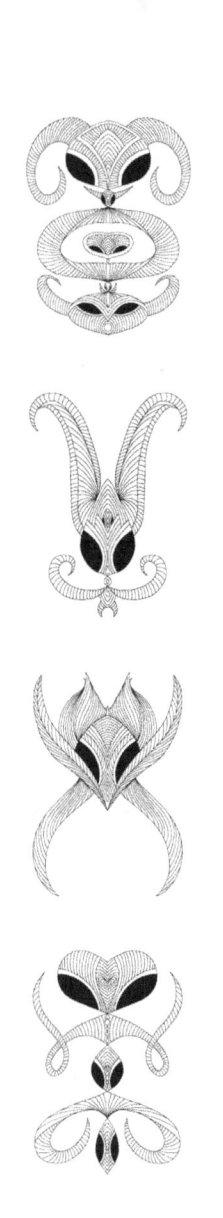
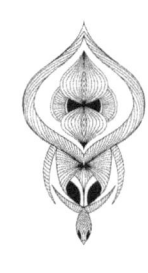
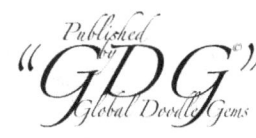

Published by
"GDG"
Global Doodle Gems

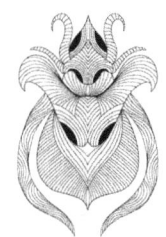

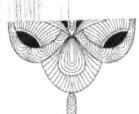
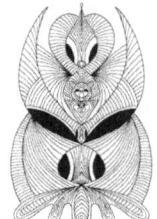
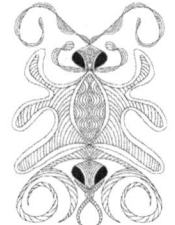
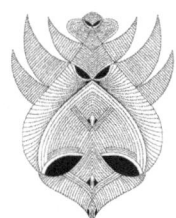
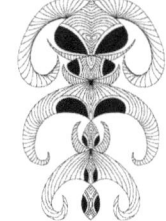
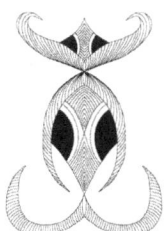
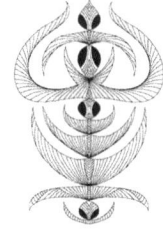
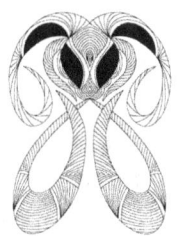
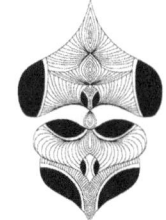

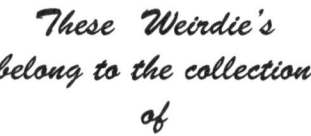

These Weirdie's belong to the collection of

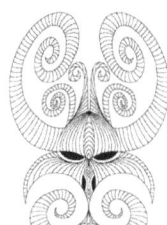
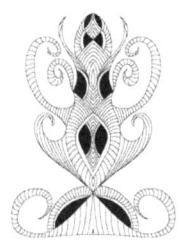
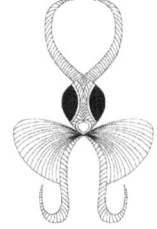
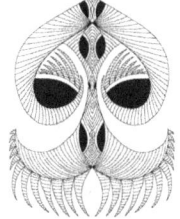
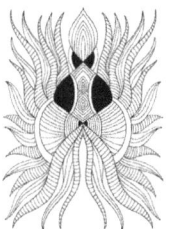
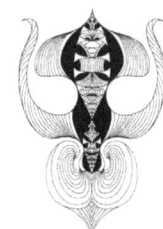
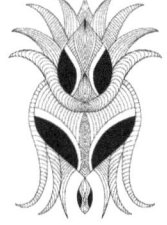
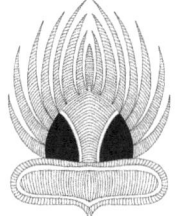
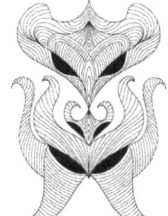
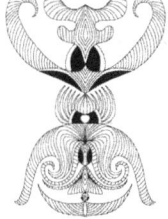
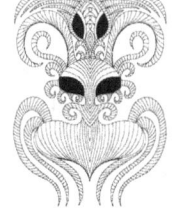
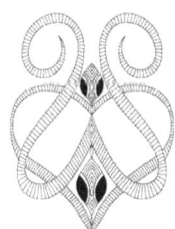
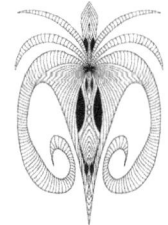
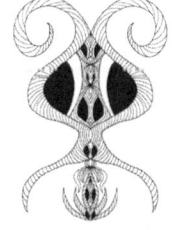
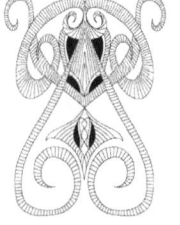
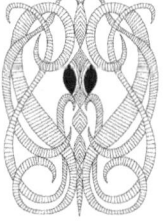

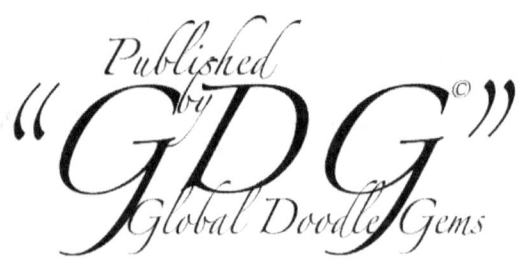

Share your colored versions with us! We love seeing your results and hearing from you we are social!

The Official FB book page, stay on top of what we have in the works!
www.facebook.com/globaldoodlegems
The Community group, share your colored pages, meet the artists, enjoy exclusive freebies, take part in community Charity books and so much more......
www.facebook.com/groups/globaldoodlegems/
Follow us on Twitter.... @GlobalDoodlegem
We are on Instagram too
@globaldoodlegems for instagram
...and if you are not social like that we have a blog
globaldoodlegems.wordpress.com

Copyright © 2019 Global Doodle Gems
All rights are reserved by Global Doodle Gems.
Duplication of pages for personal use are allowed. You are invited to color the pages then scan/post your coloured versions to social networks, mentioning the book title and author/artist (Global Doodle Gems).
All artwork and images are protected by copyright laws. This book or any portion thereof may not, otherwise, be reproduced and/or distributed or transmitted without the express written permission of the artist/publisher of Global Doodle Gems.
All of us from the Global Doodle Gems wish you a colortastic time and look forward to seeing your wonderful color results online!

Welcome to my world of Weirdies

This is the first weirdies book of year 3 of Color A Weirdie A Day, join us for daily coloring with either me or one of the wonderful guesthosts at the group www.facebook.com/groups/ColorAWeirdieADay, and check out all the beautiful colored !
The set has 12 books Weirdies 25 to Weirdies 36, one book for each month with a Weirdie for each day, additionally all Weirdies are repeated in the back of the book in their upside_down versions ...
Your Weirdie can drastically change and turn in to a brand new Weirdie. Get your Weirdie on and have a fun and relaxing time with coloring it, join the group and show your colored, join the live coloring and have fun with us ... if you like !

Weirdies 1 to 12 were colored live in 2018 January 1st to December 31st
Weirdies 13 to 24 were colored live in 2019 January 1st to December 31st
Weirdies 25 will be colored in January 2020 Daily

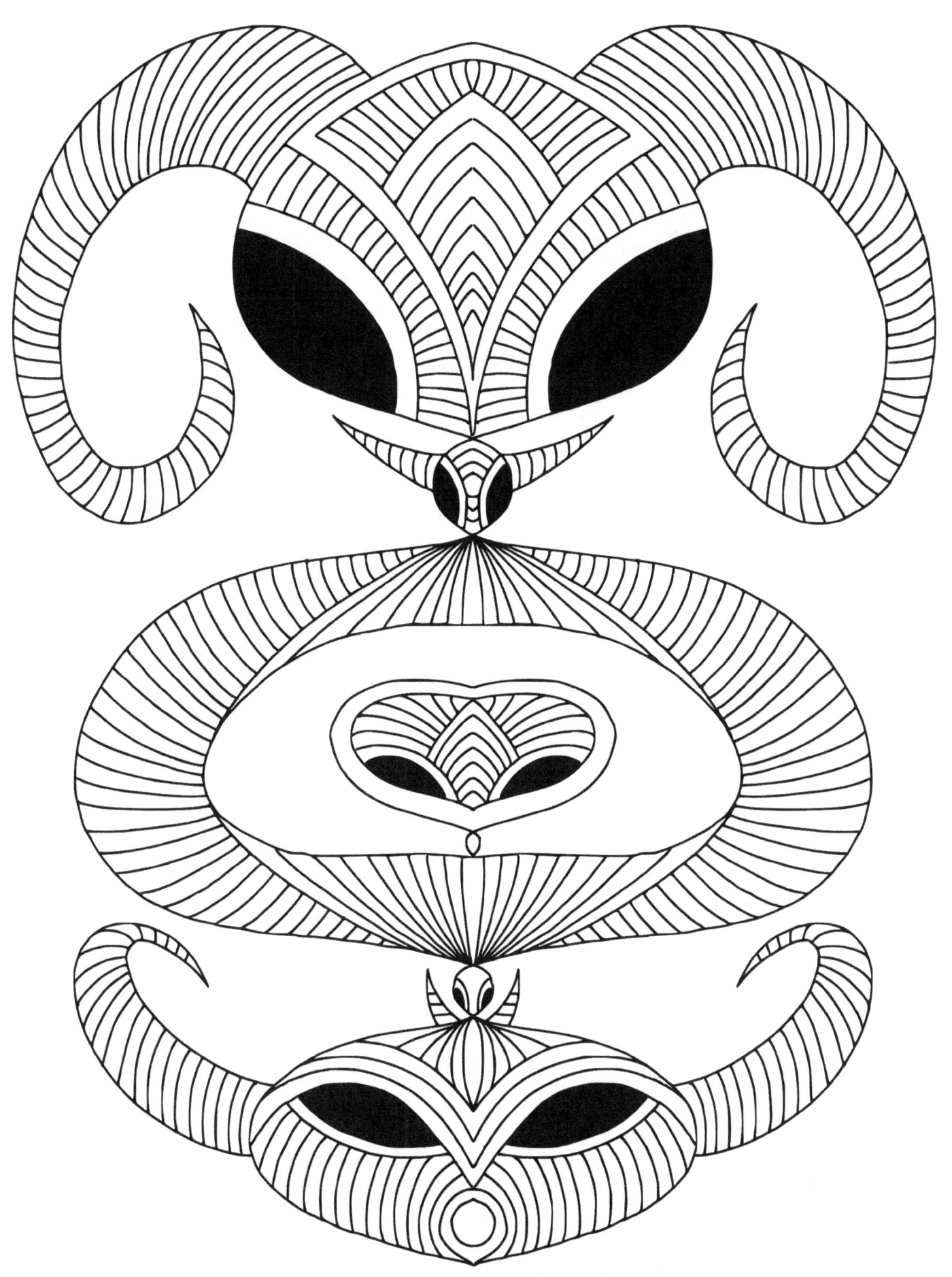

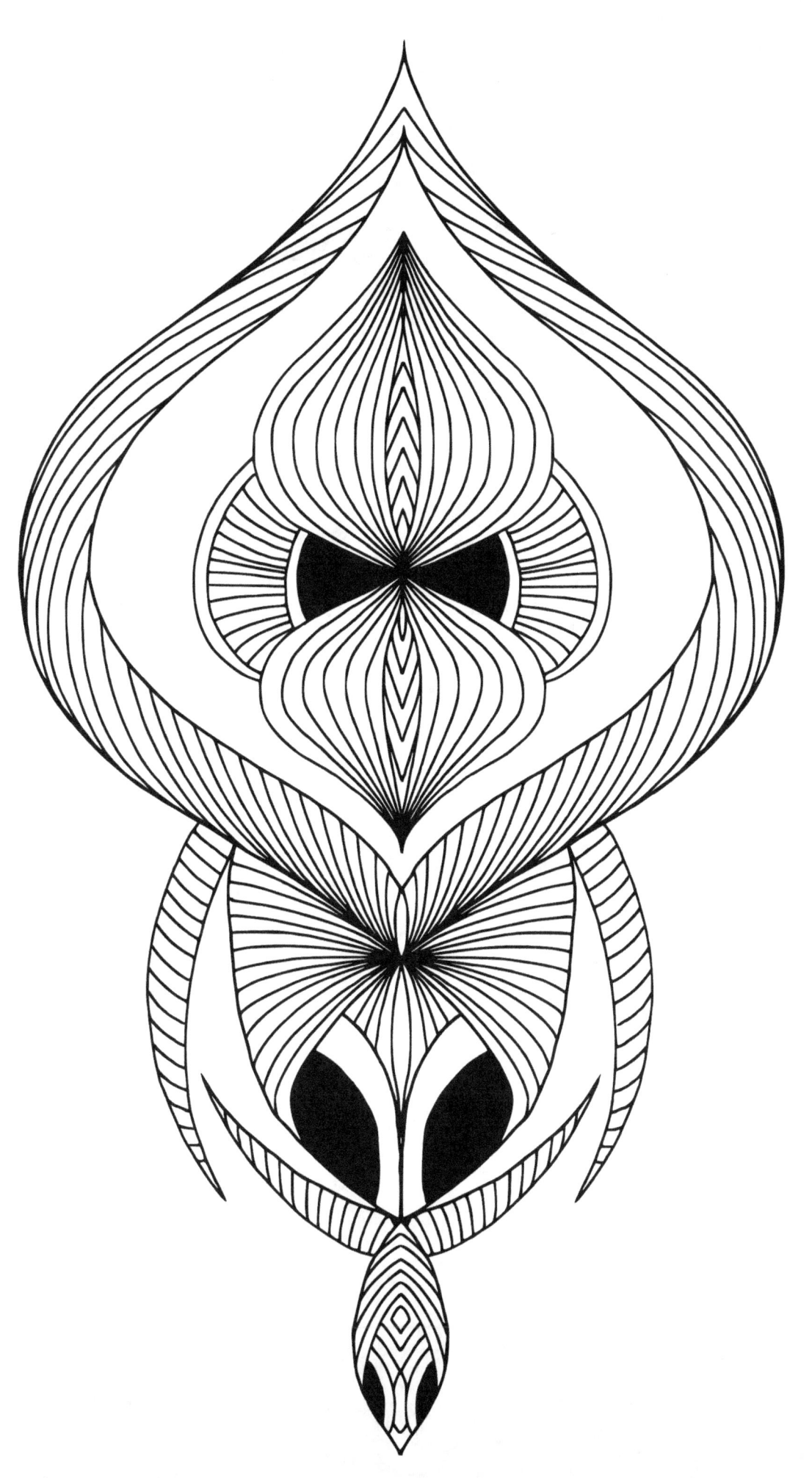

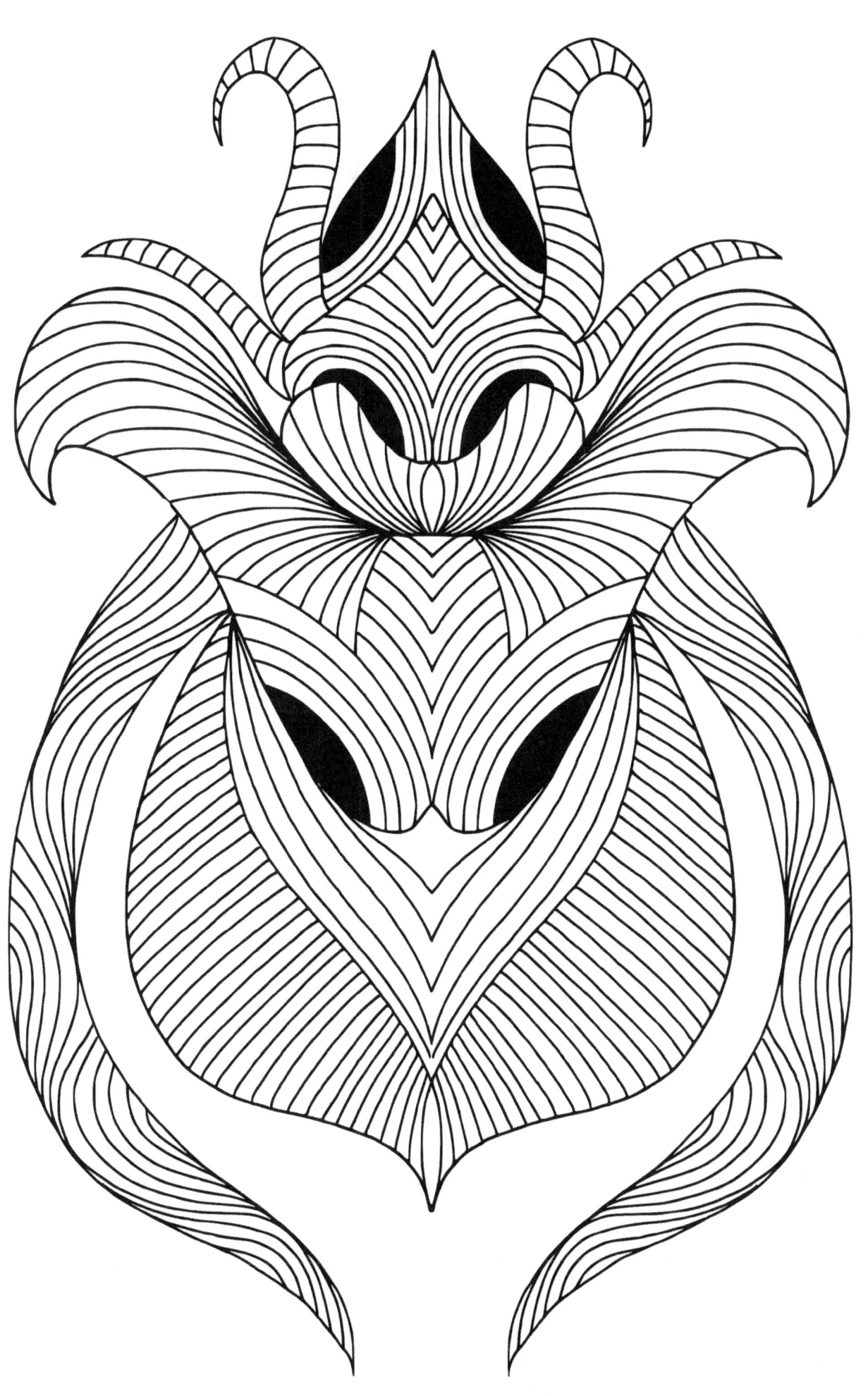

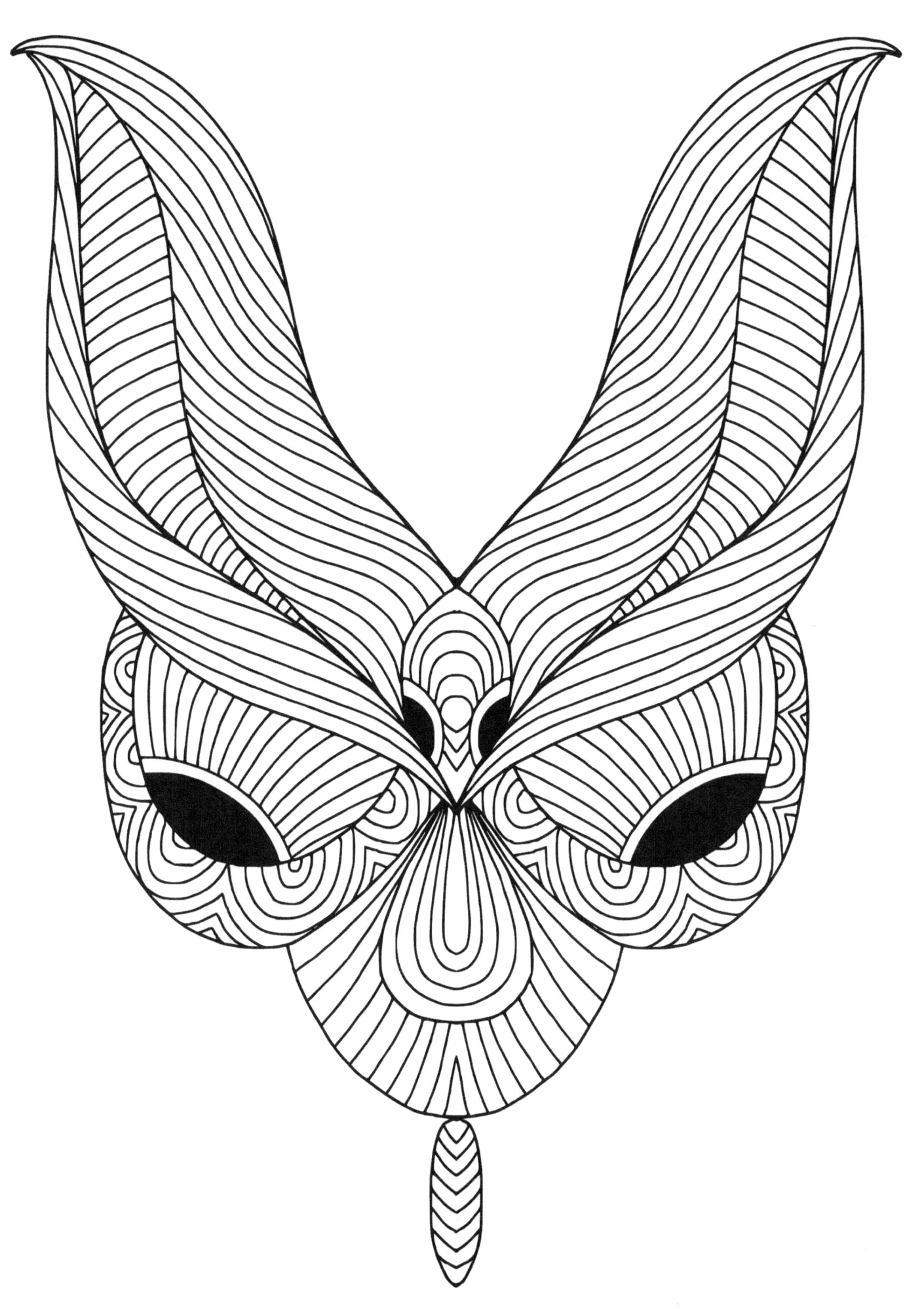

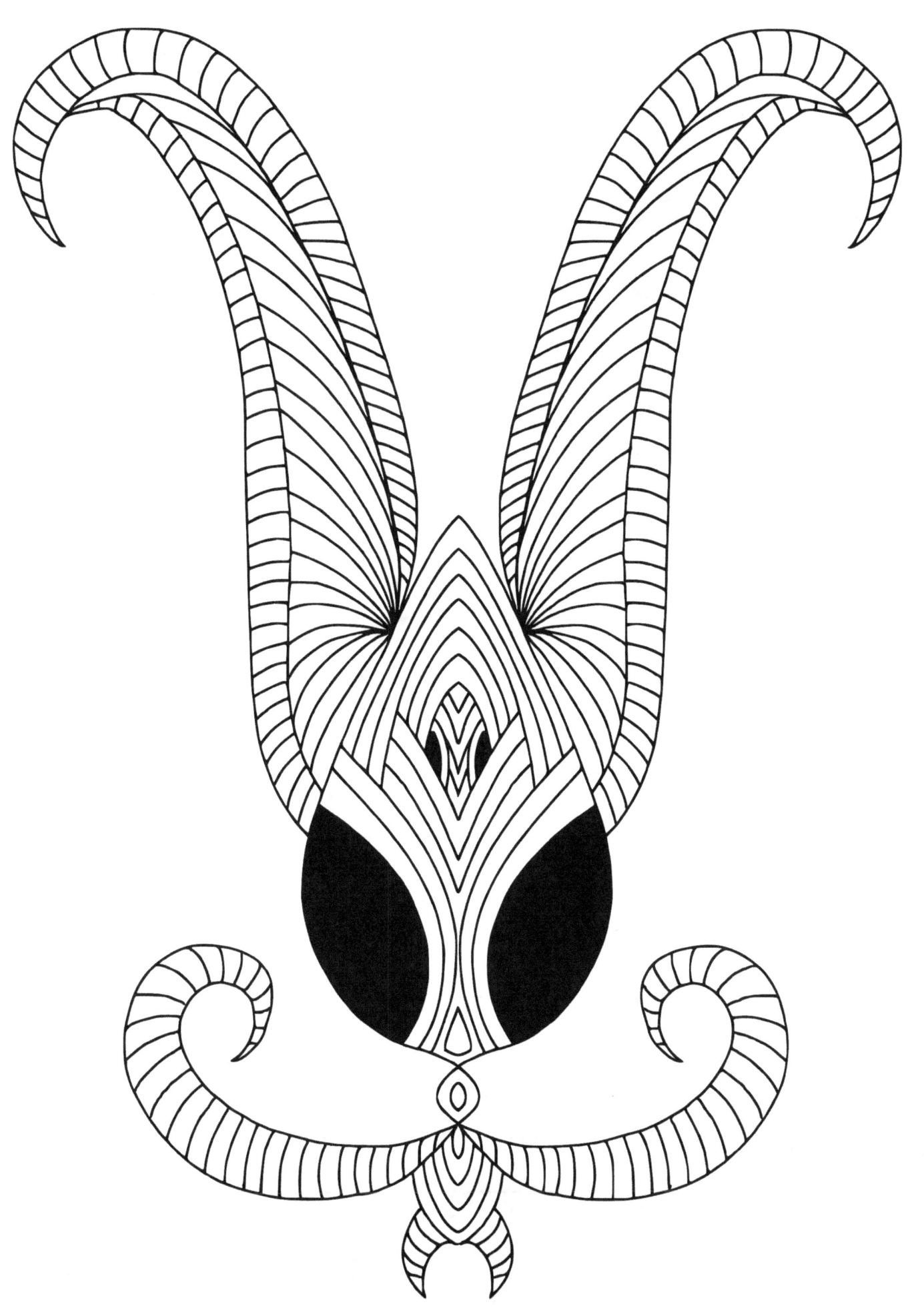

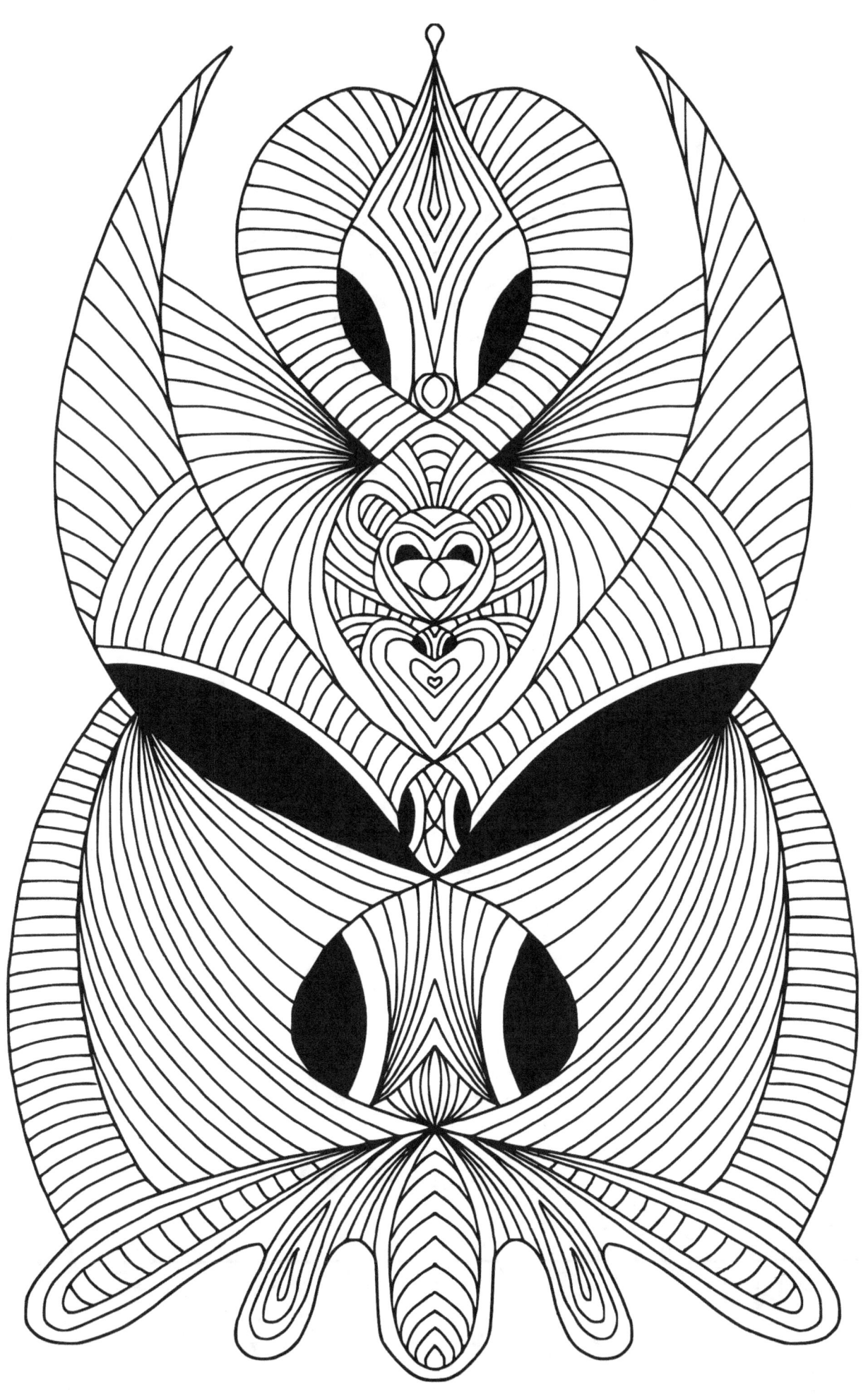

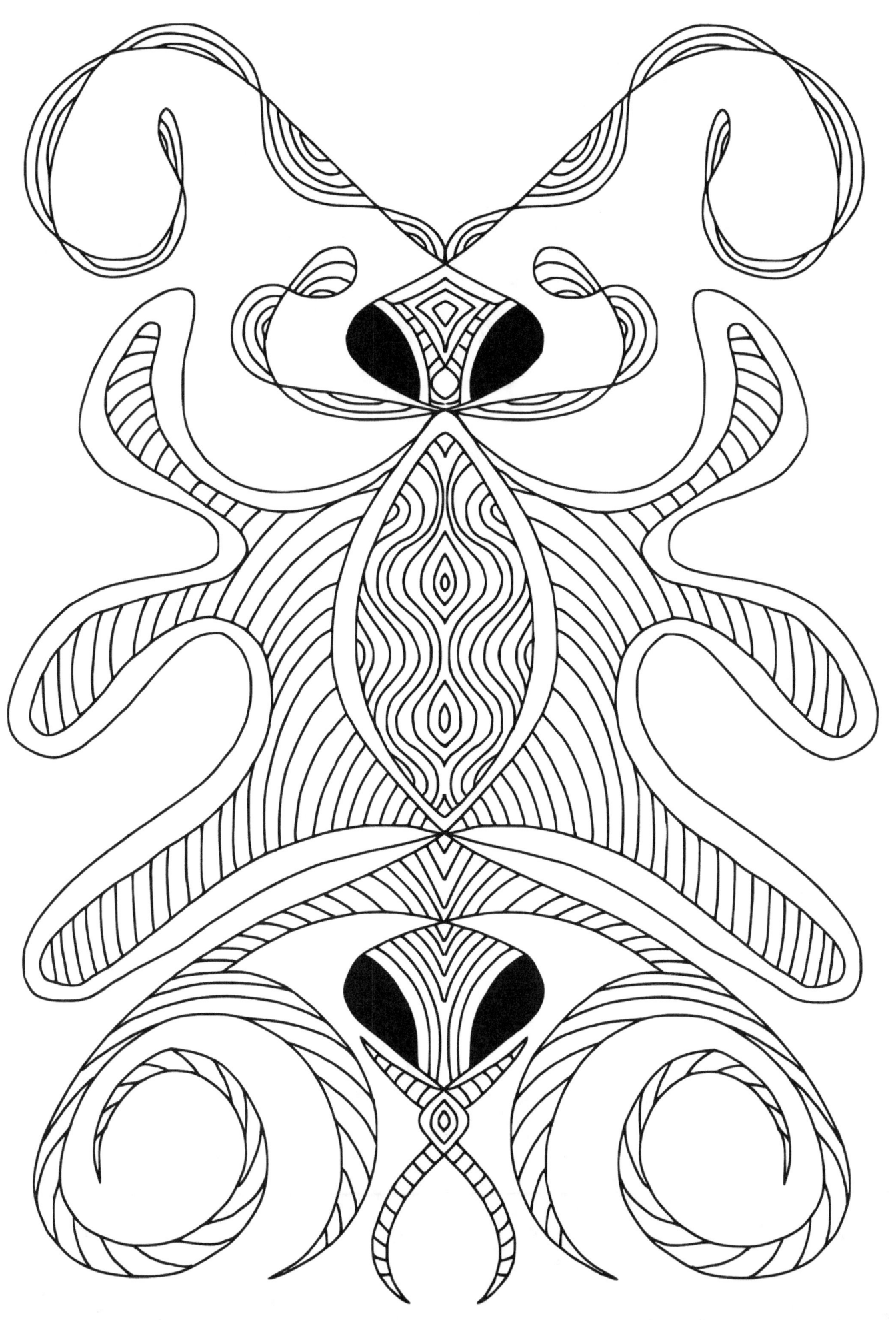

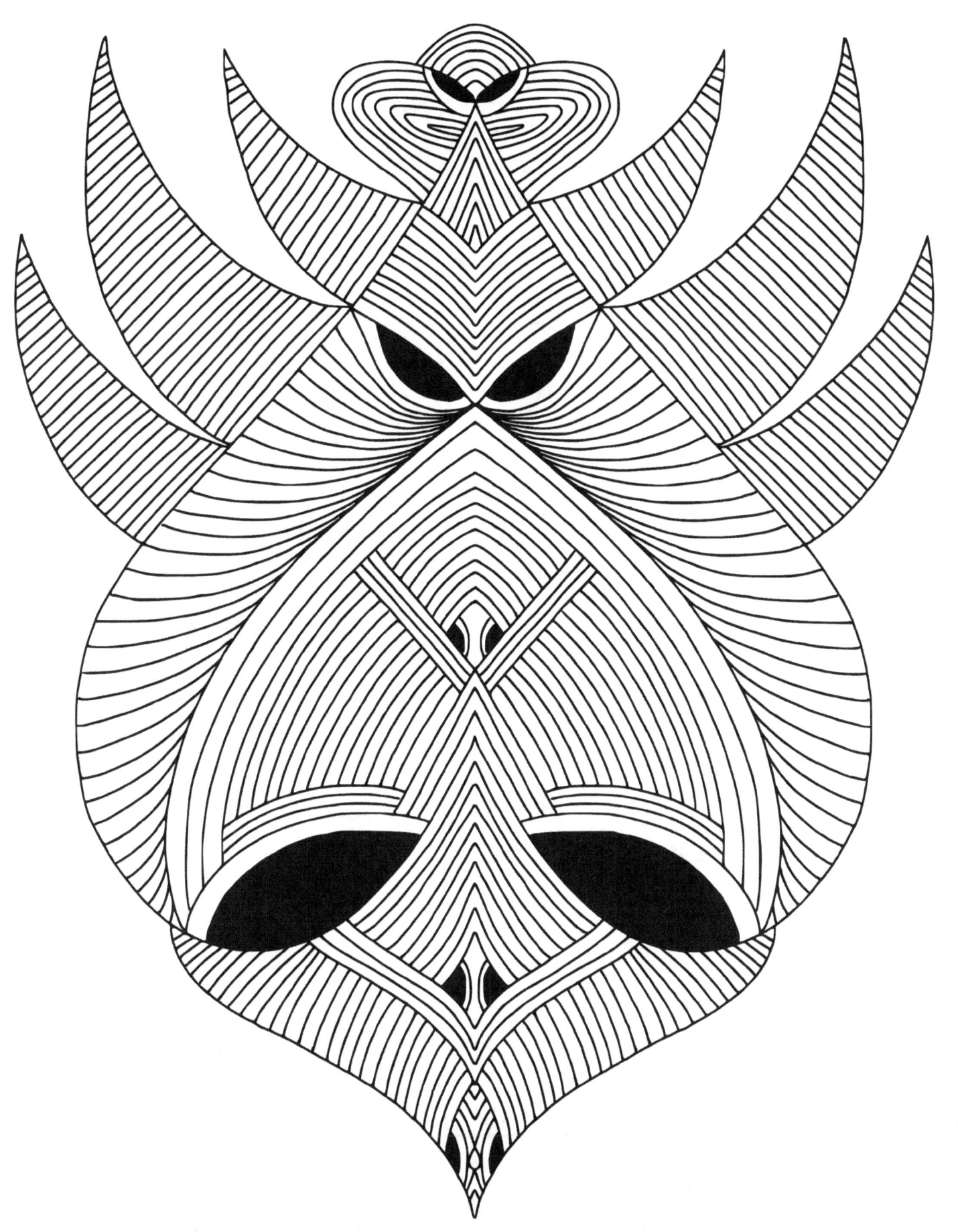

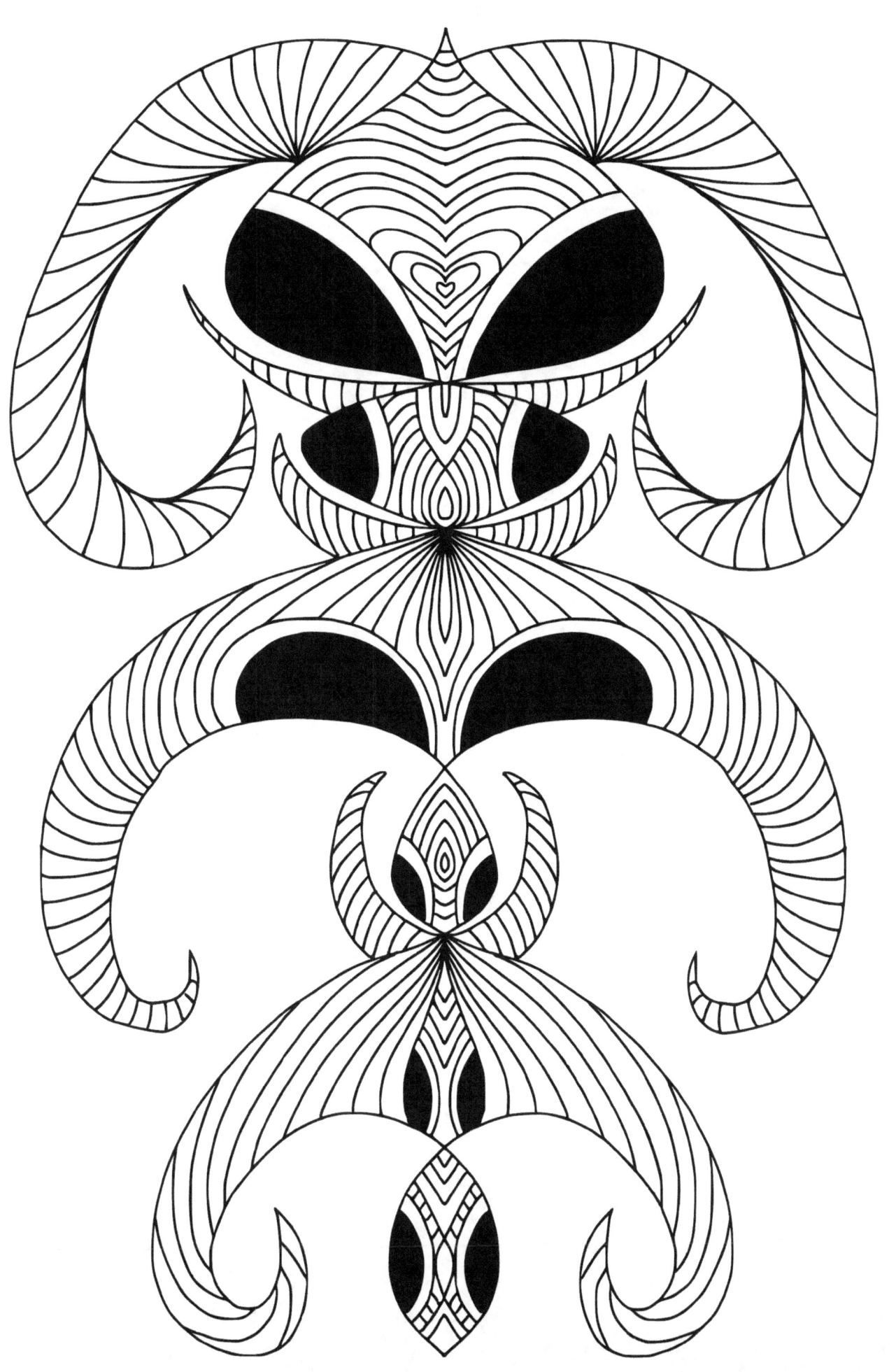

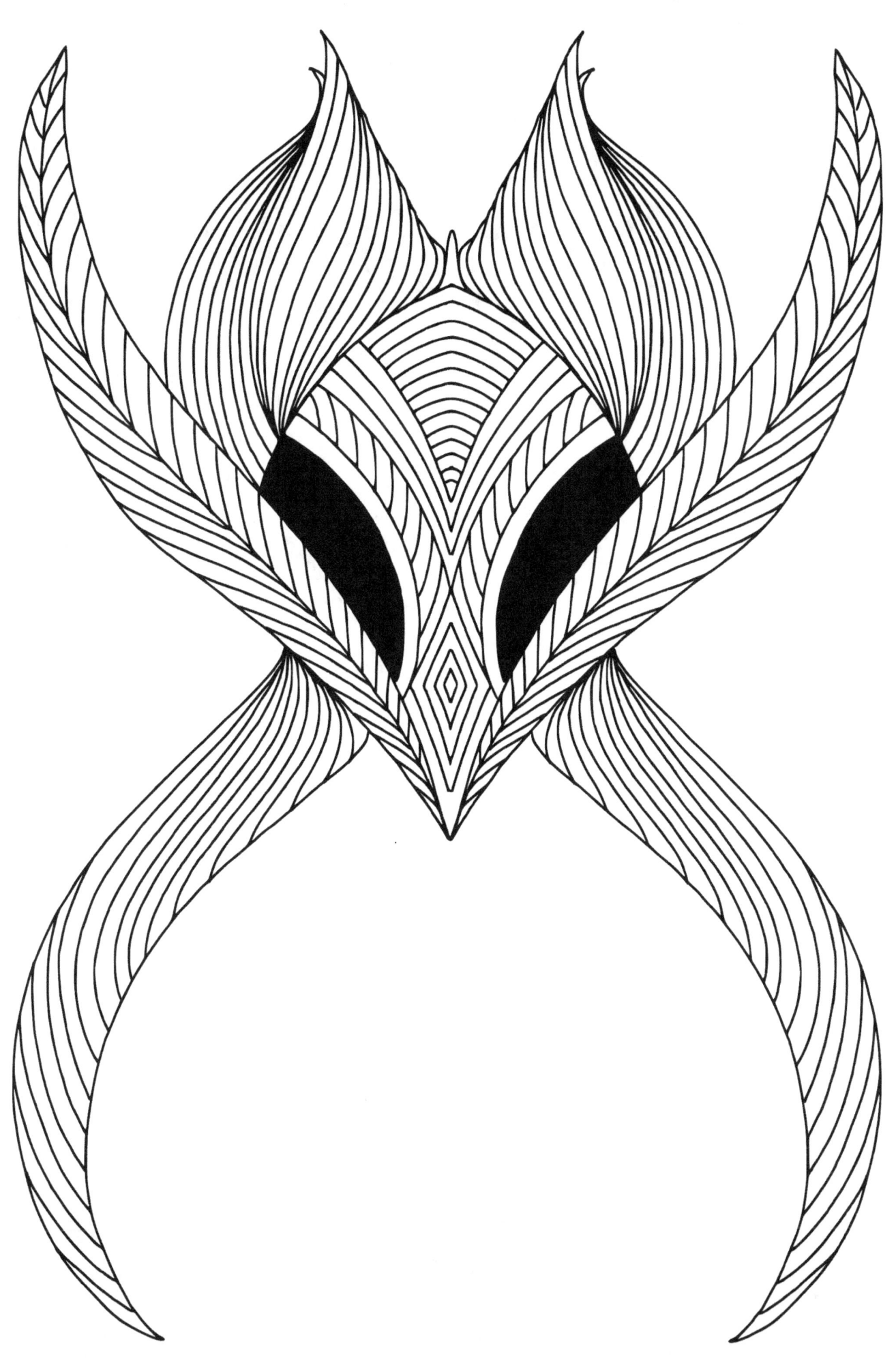

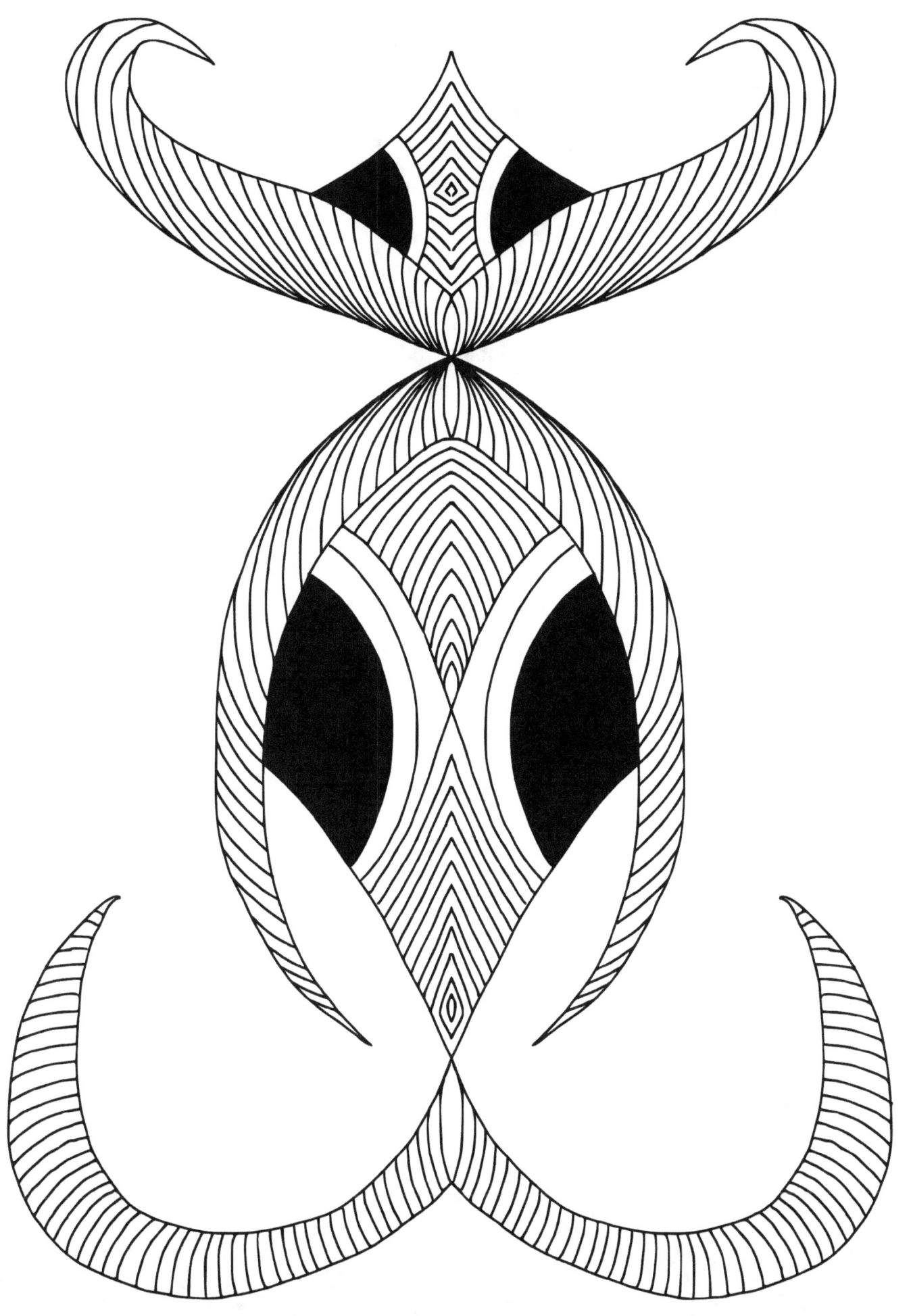

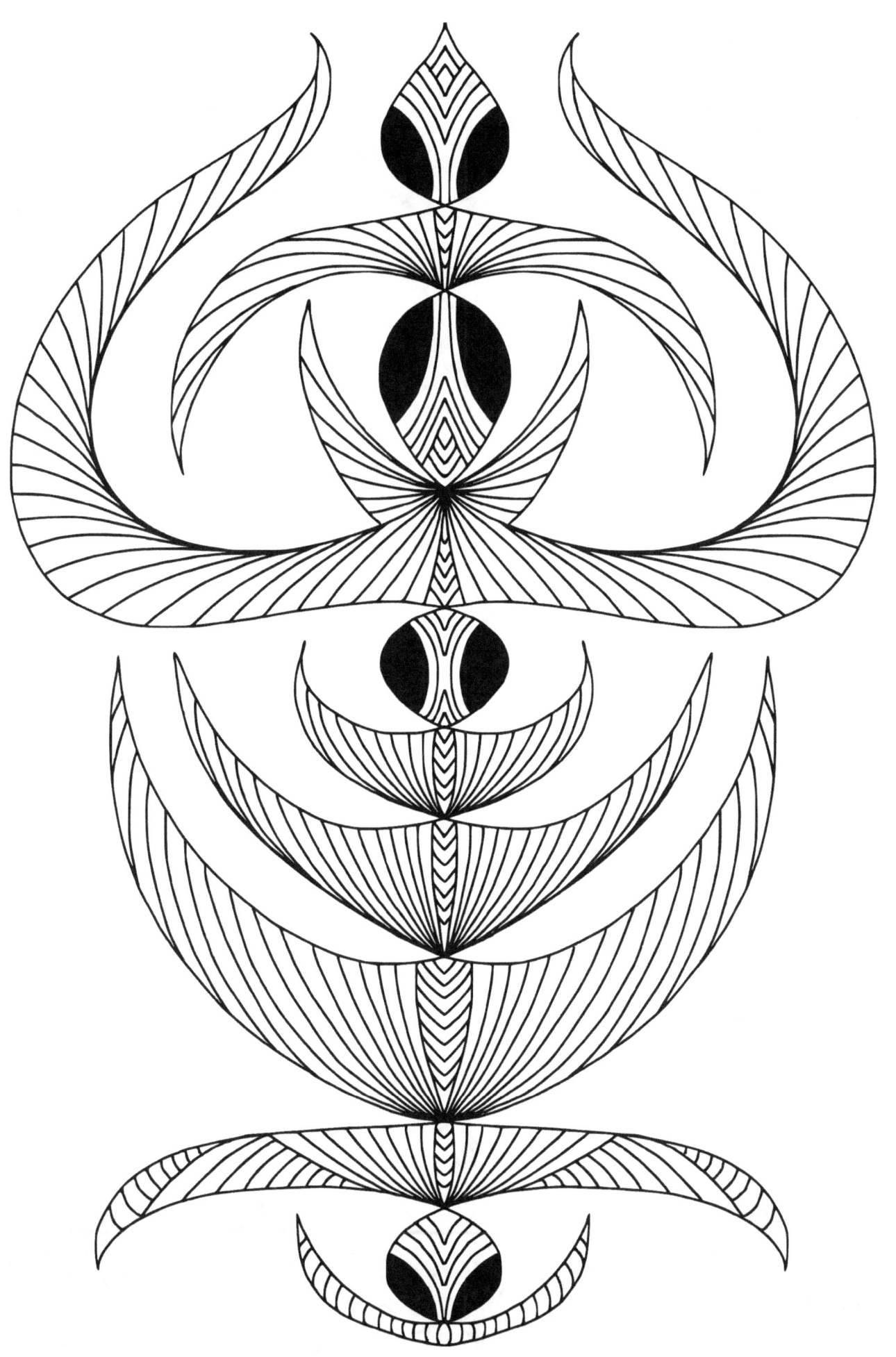

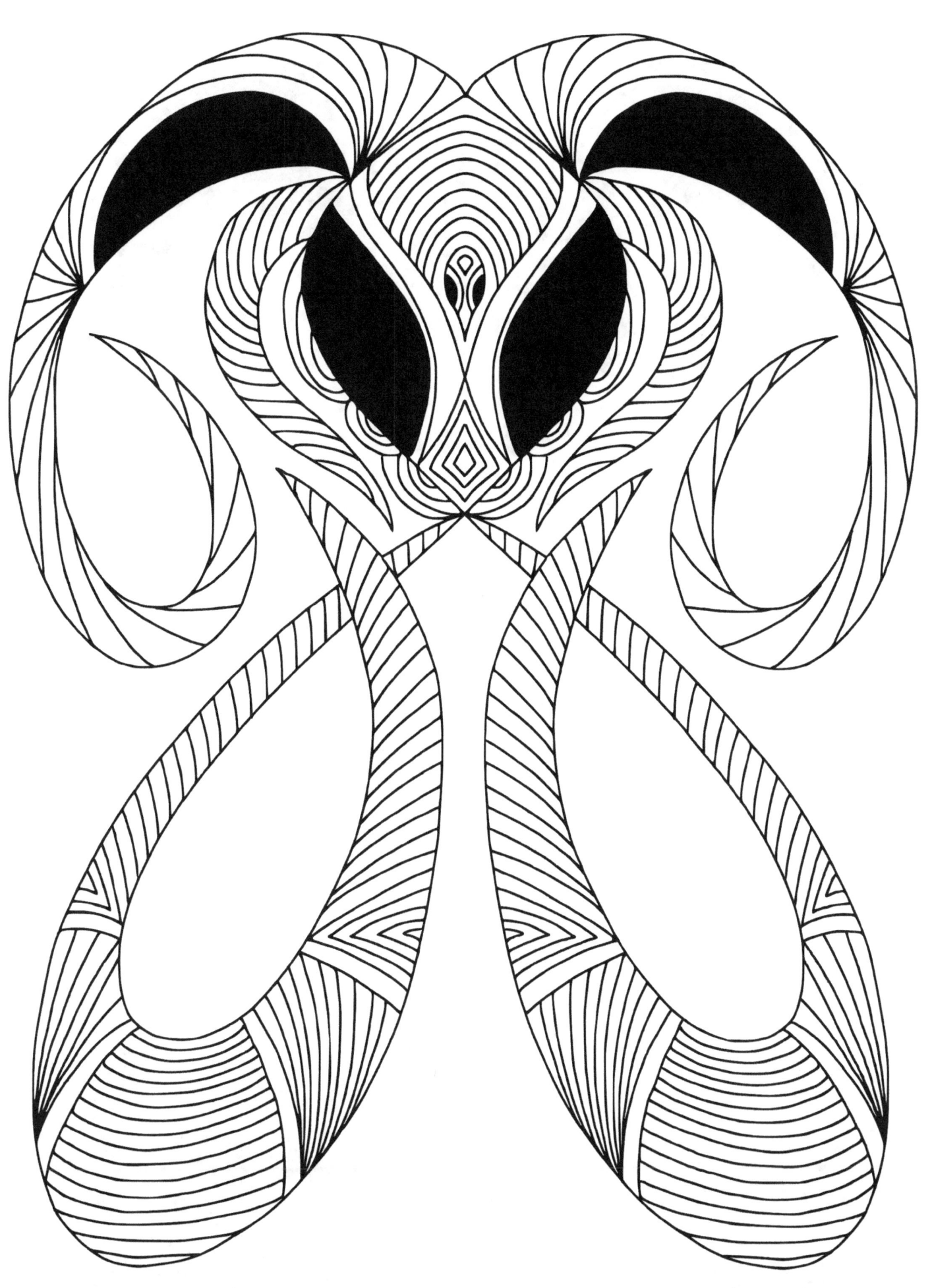

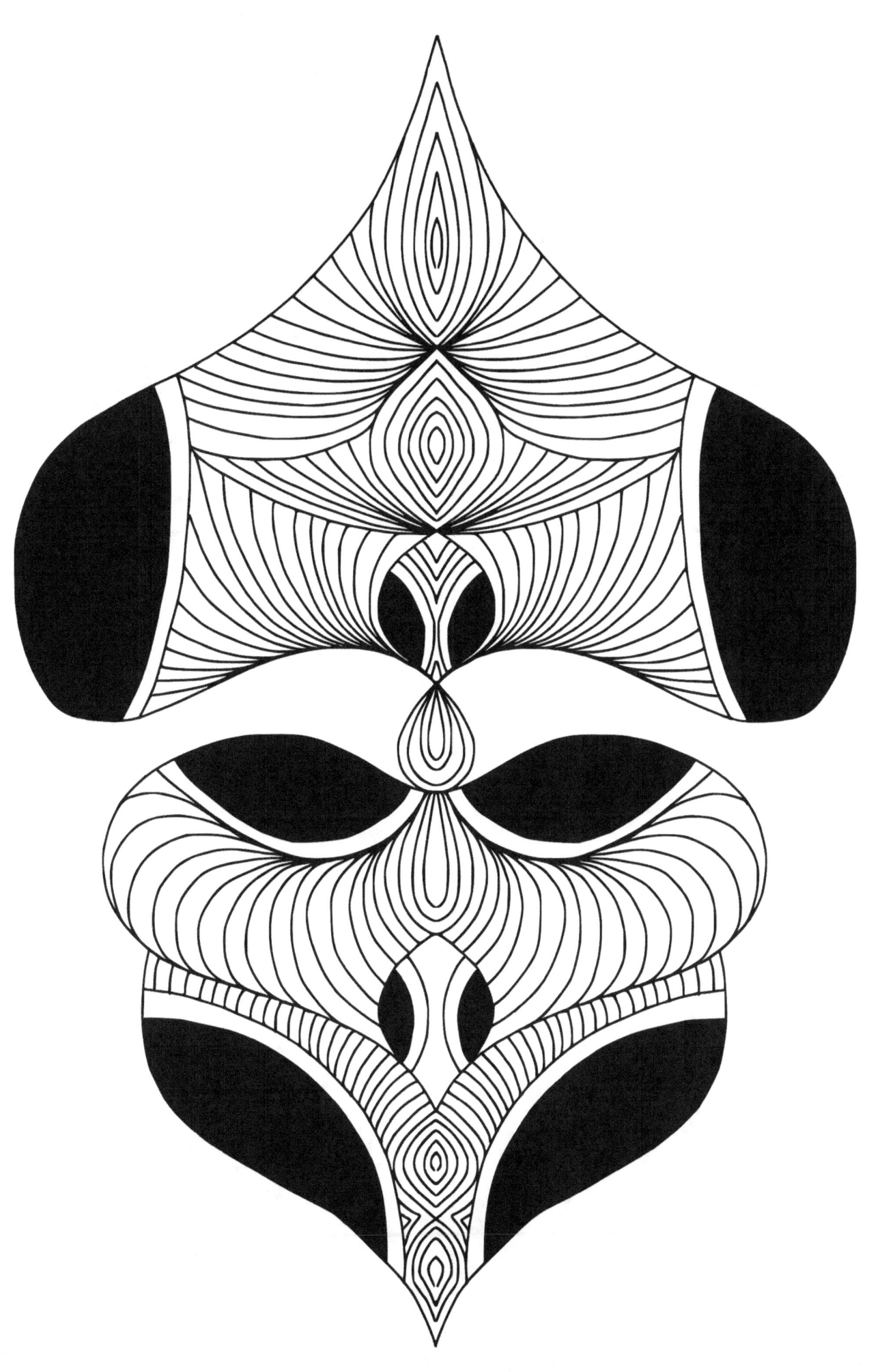

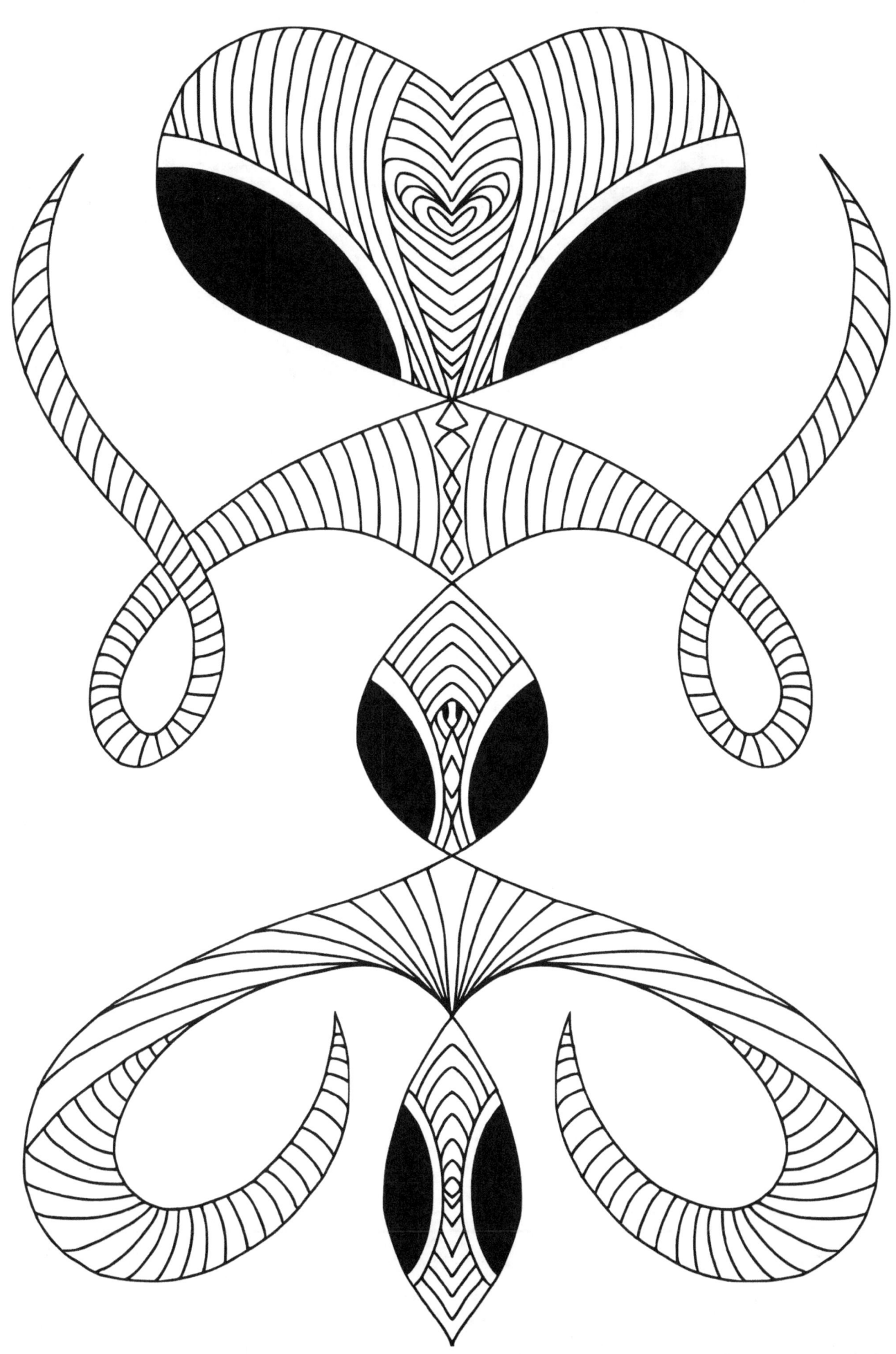

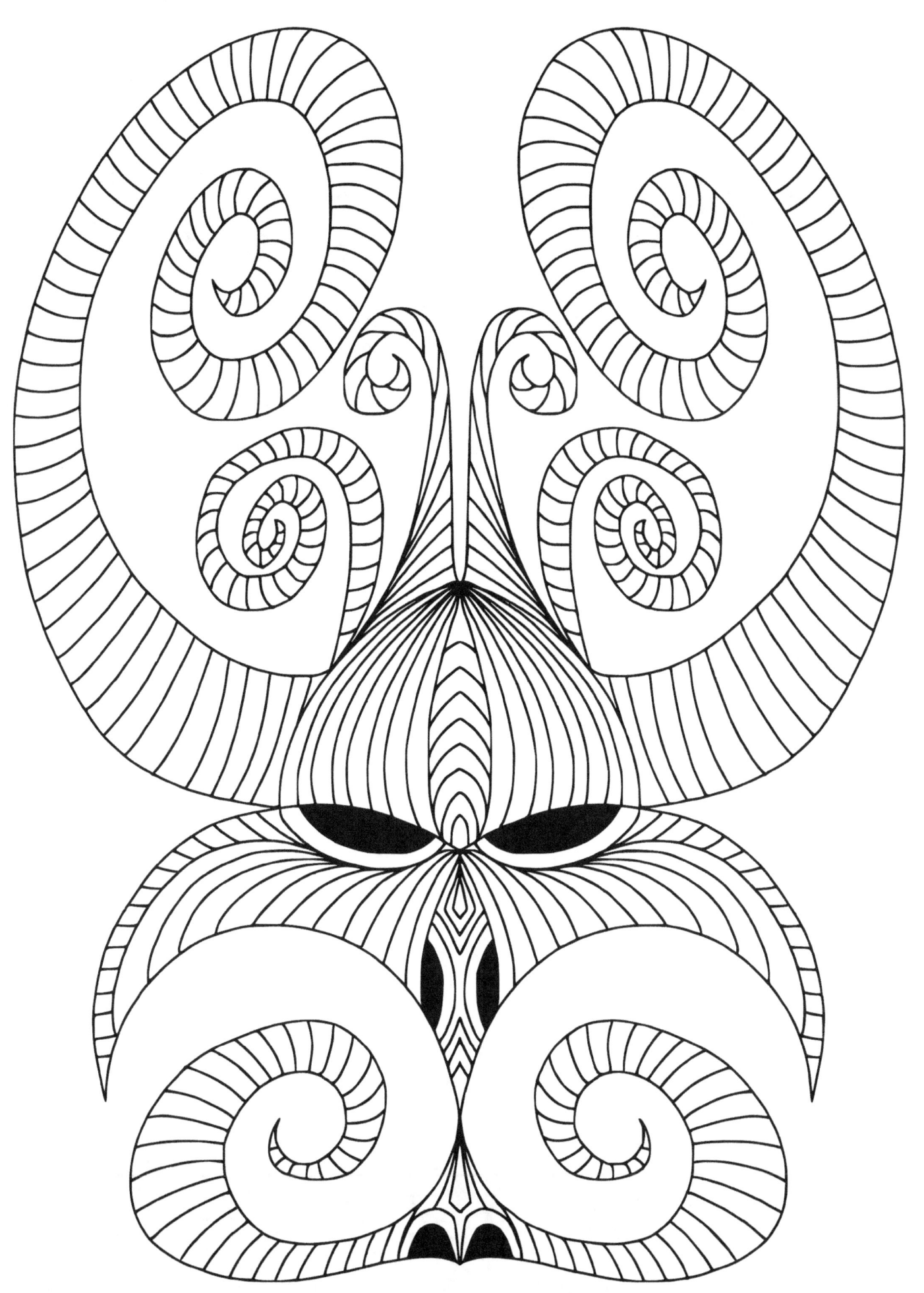

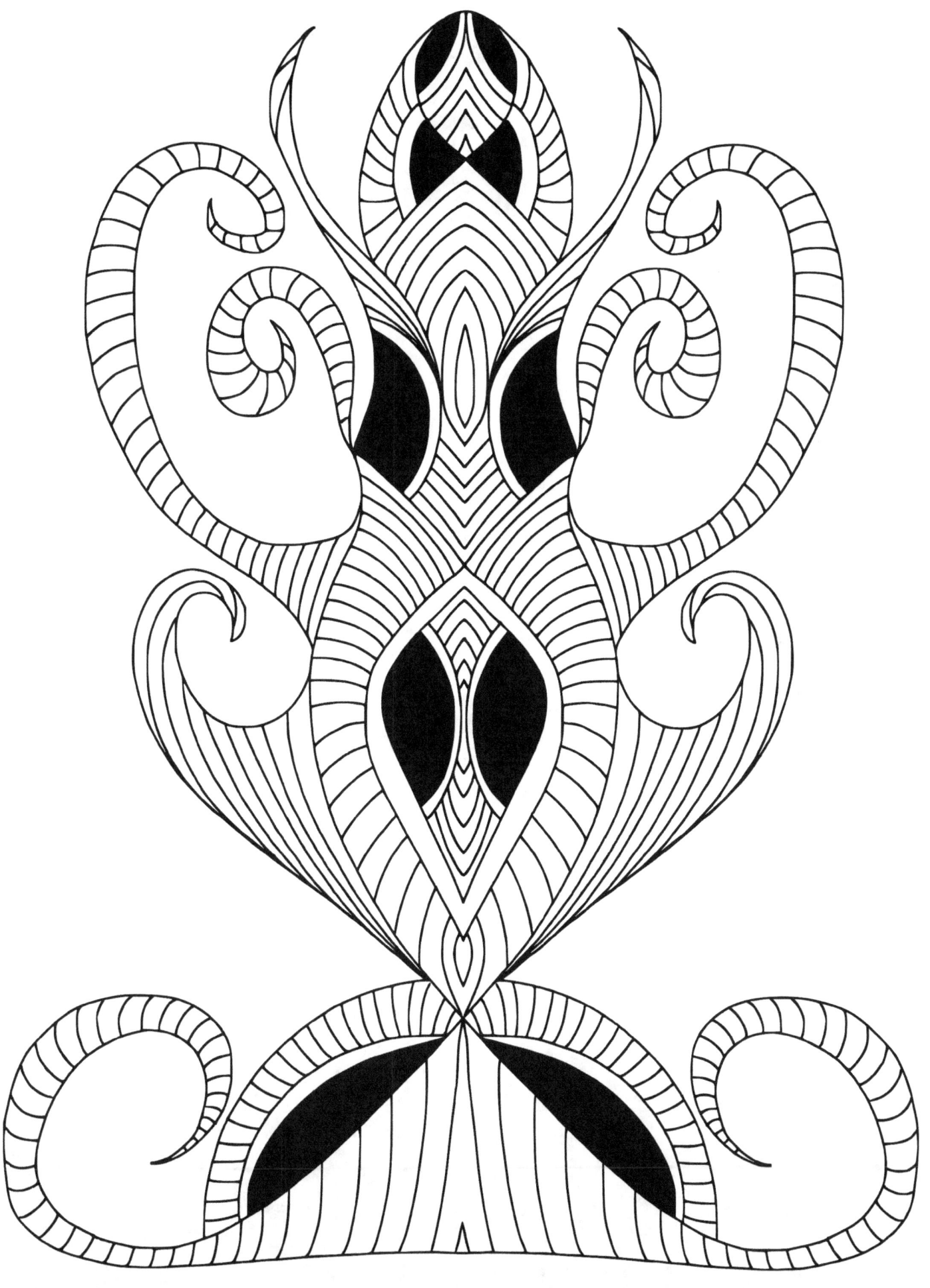

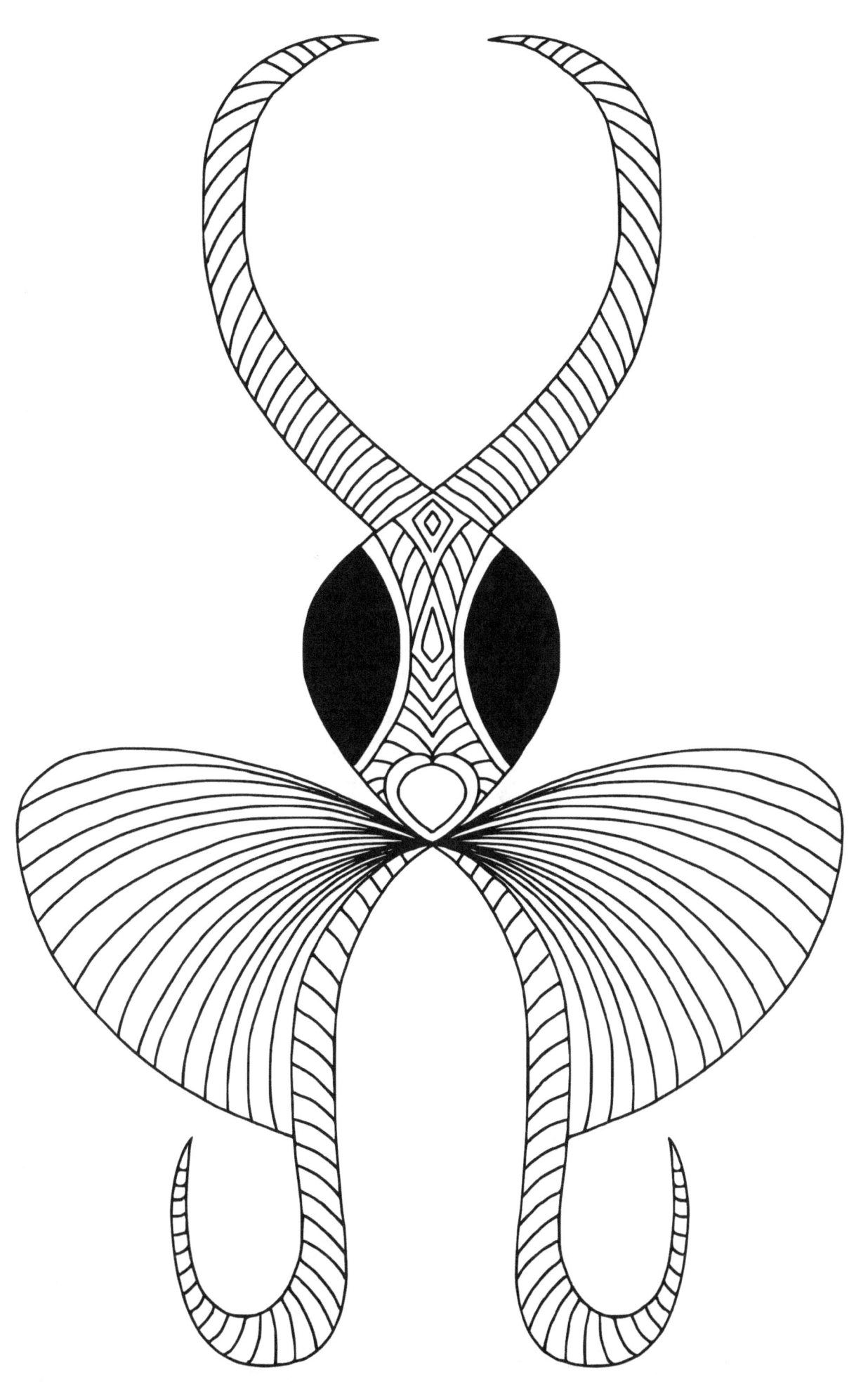

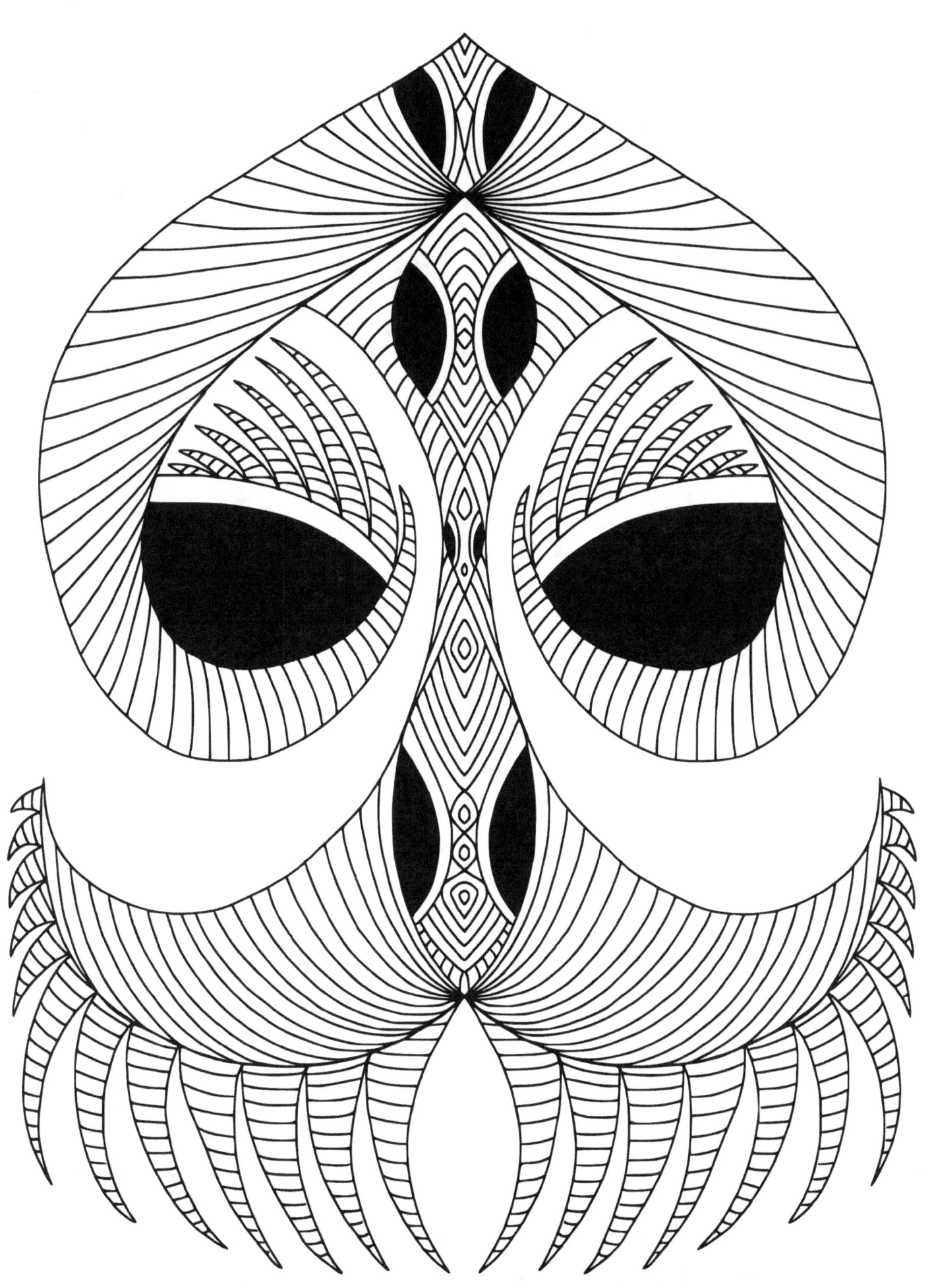

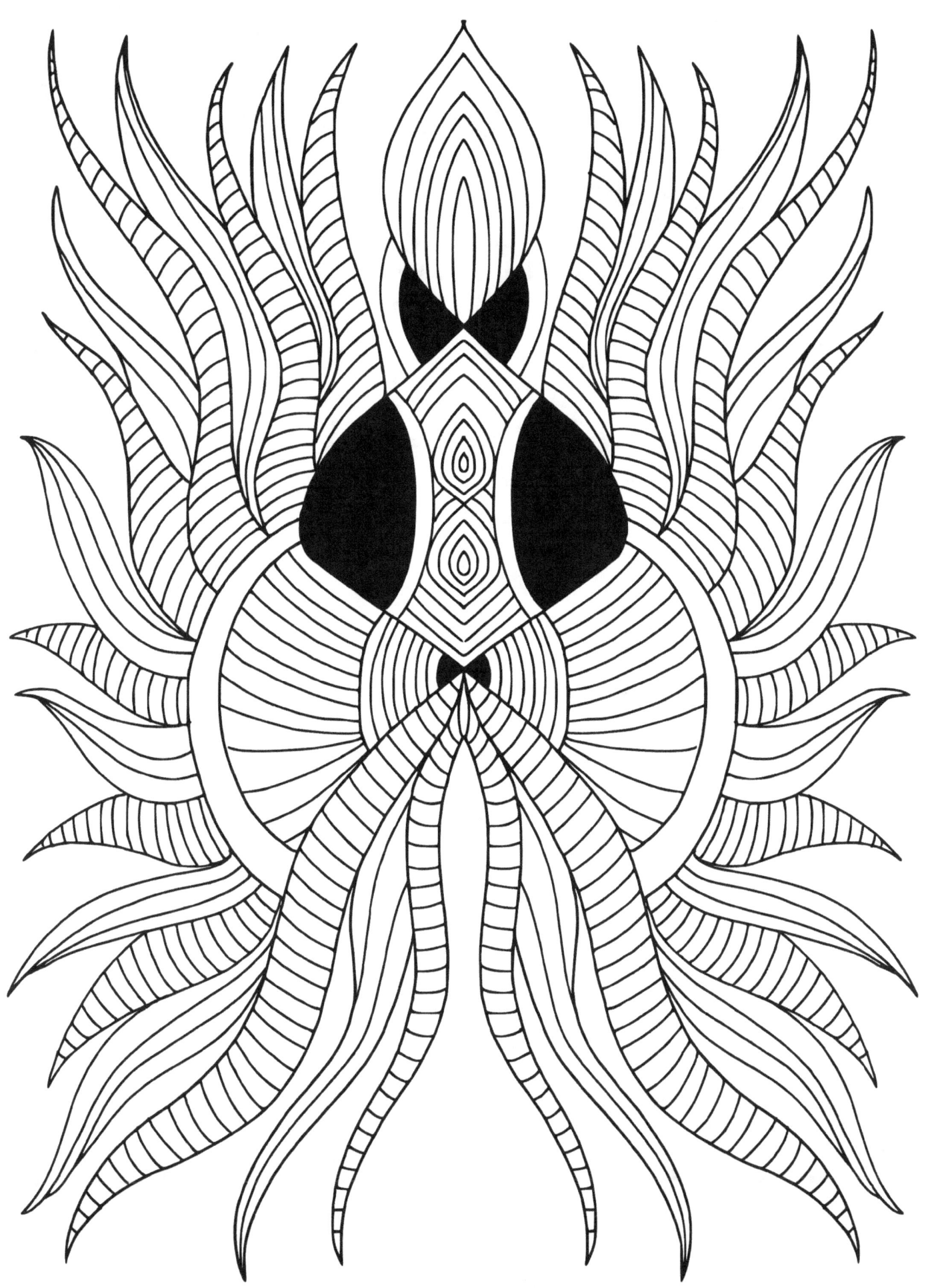

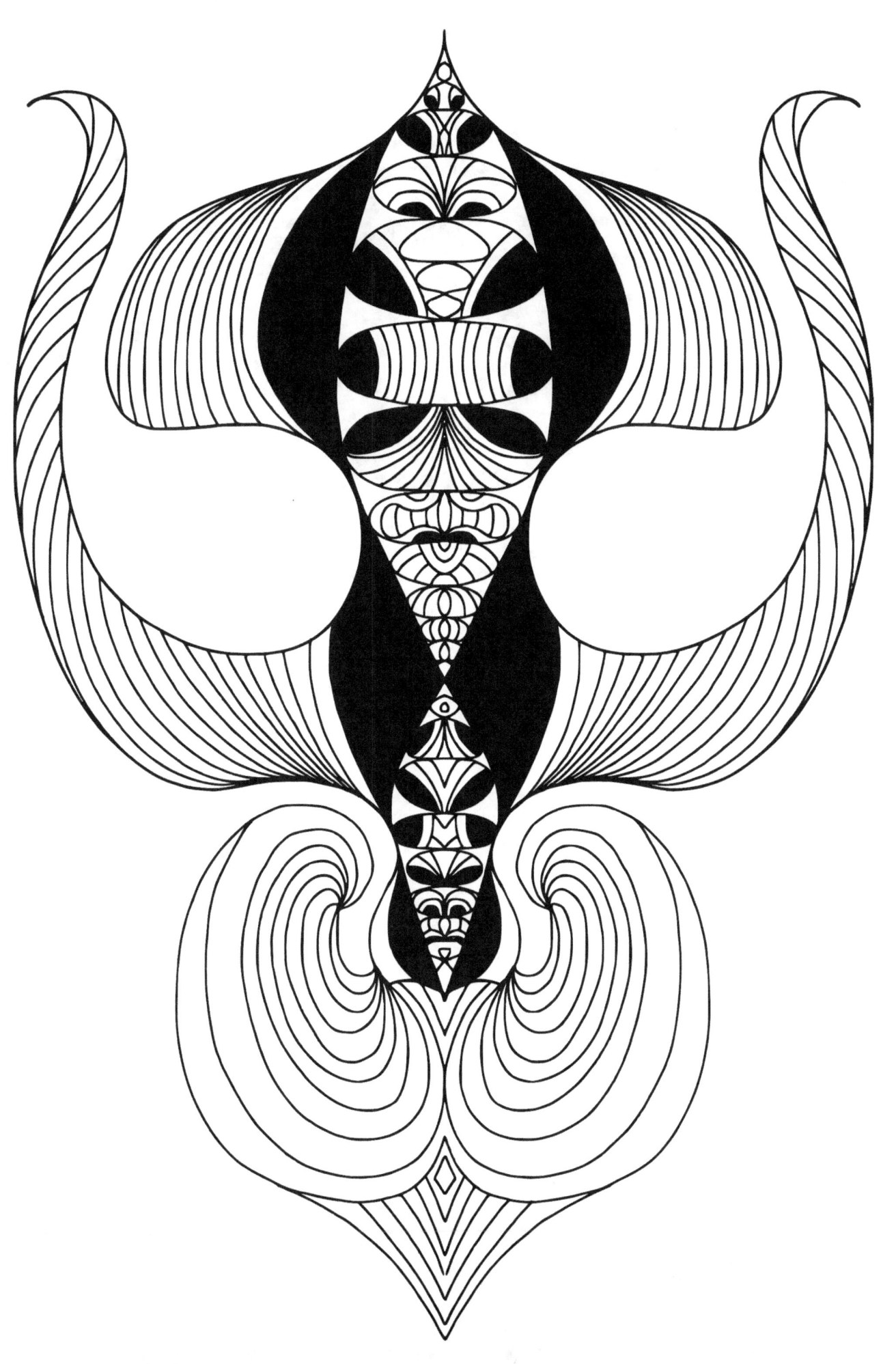

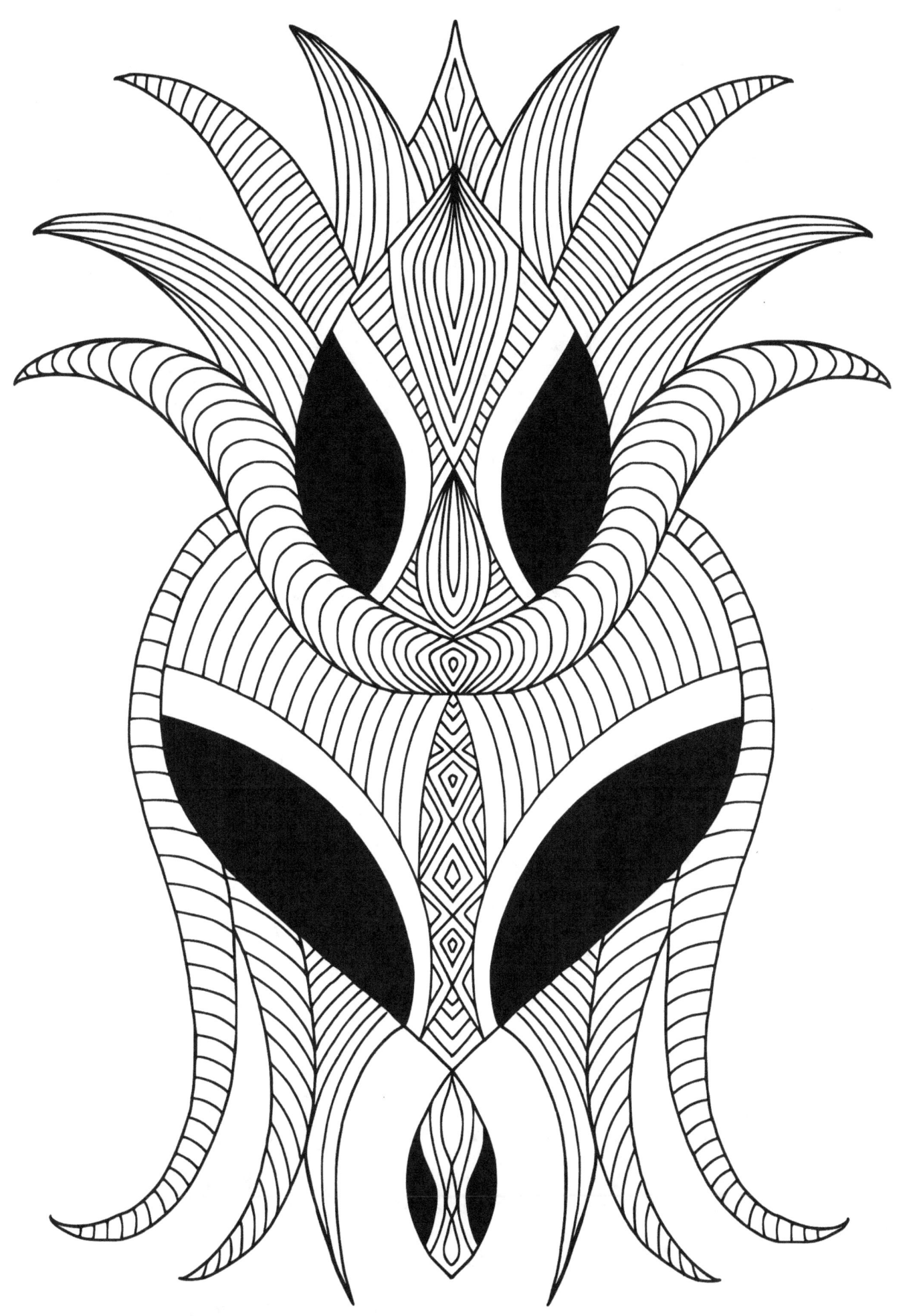

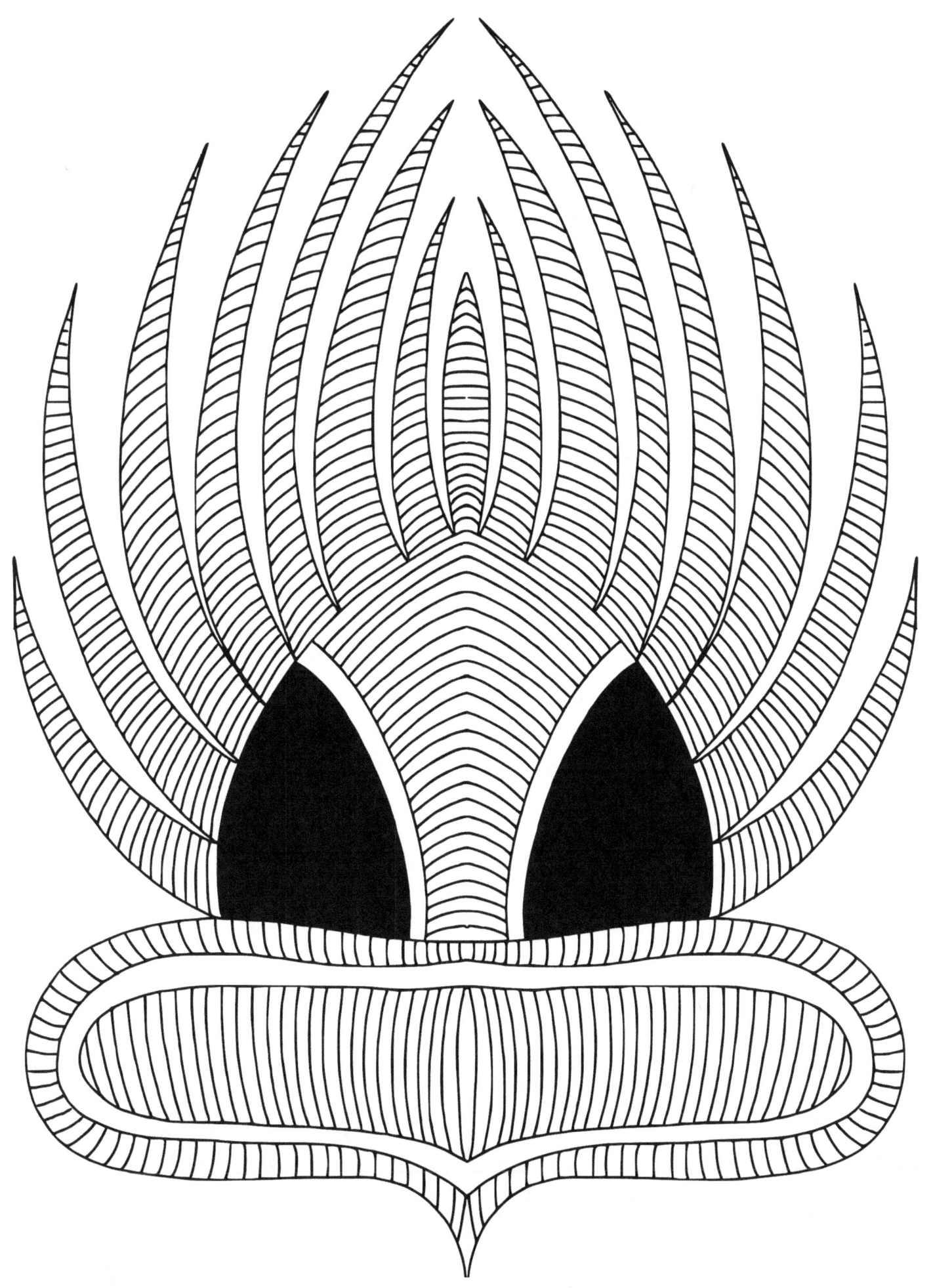

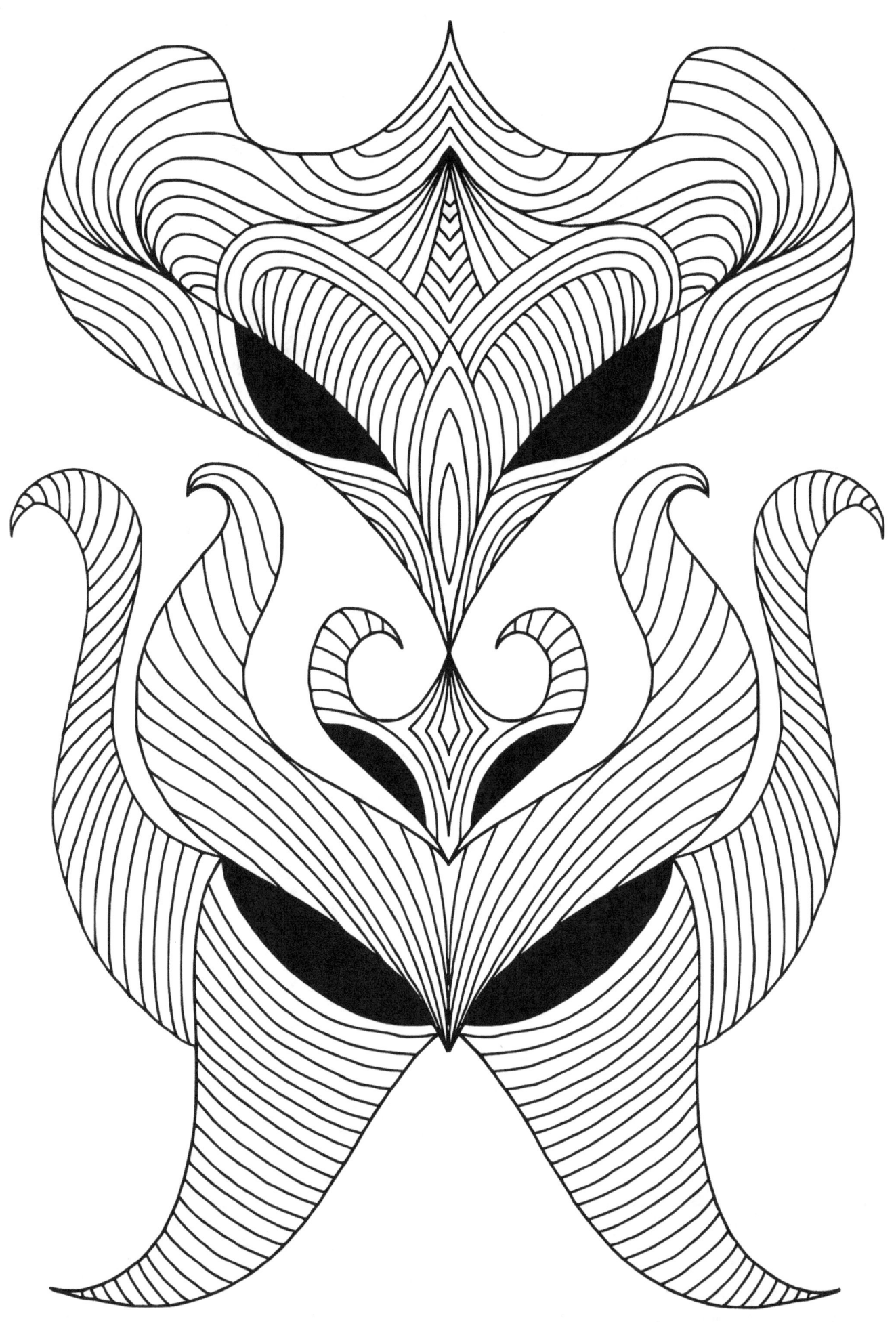

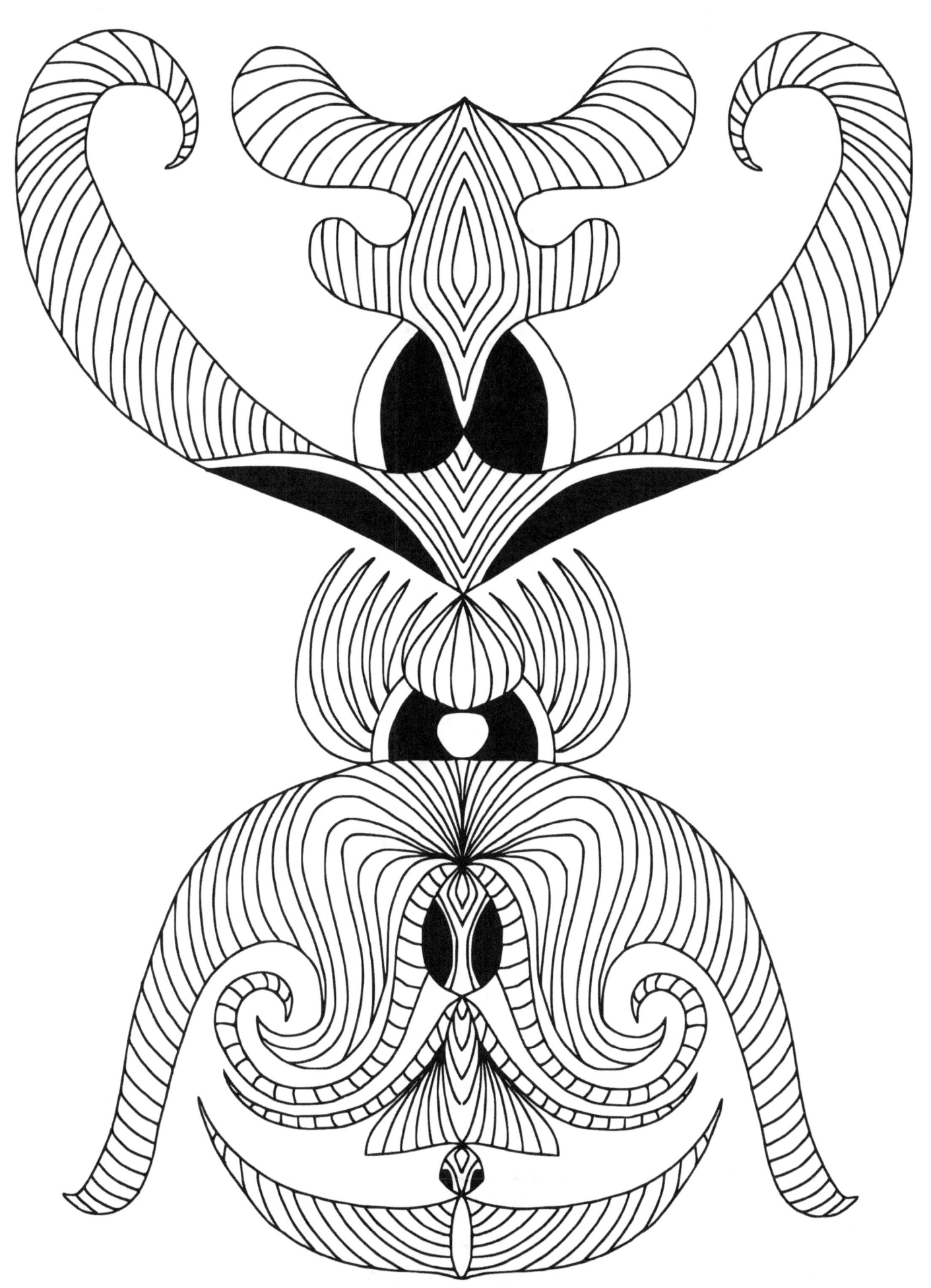

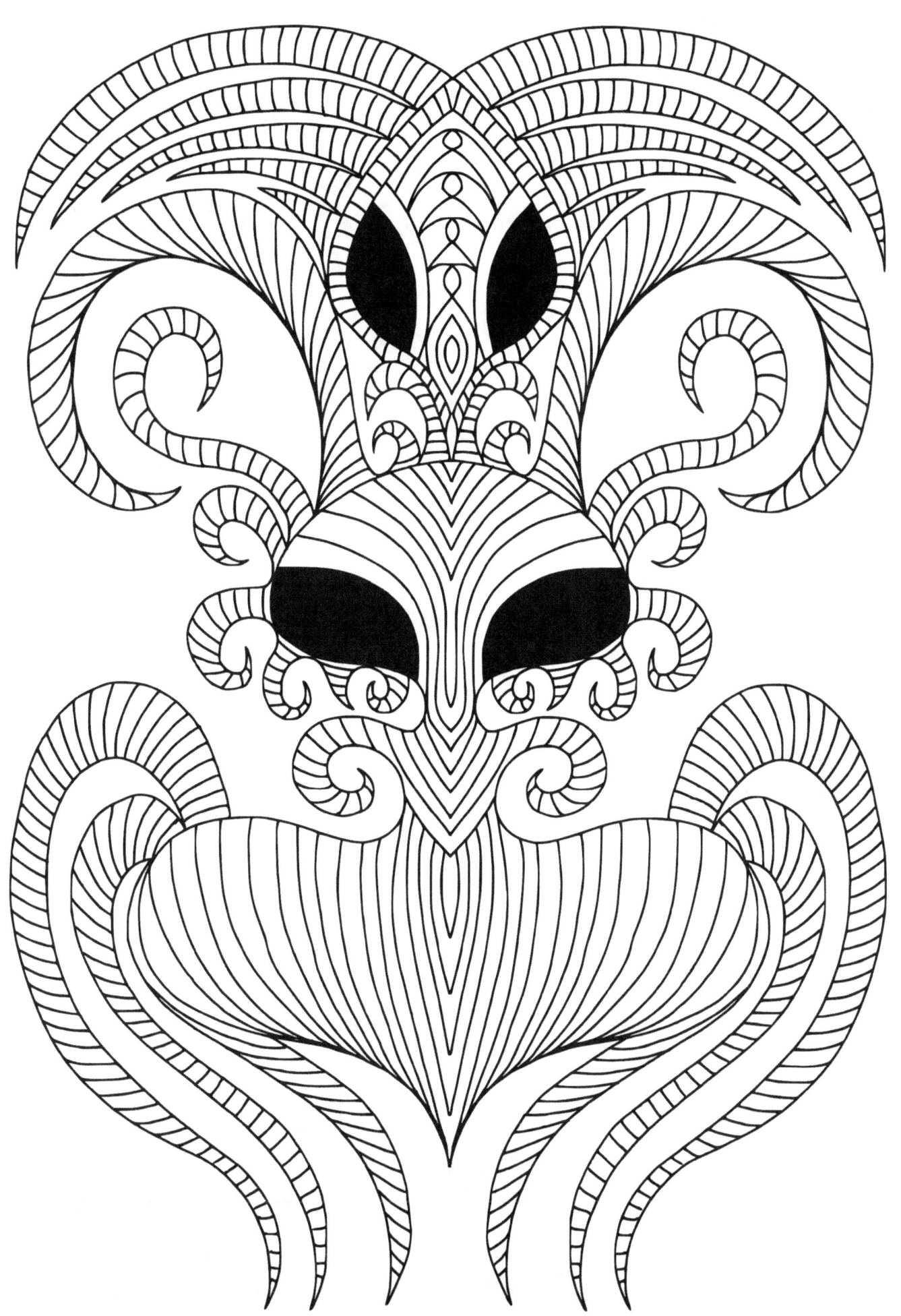

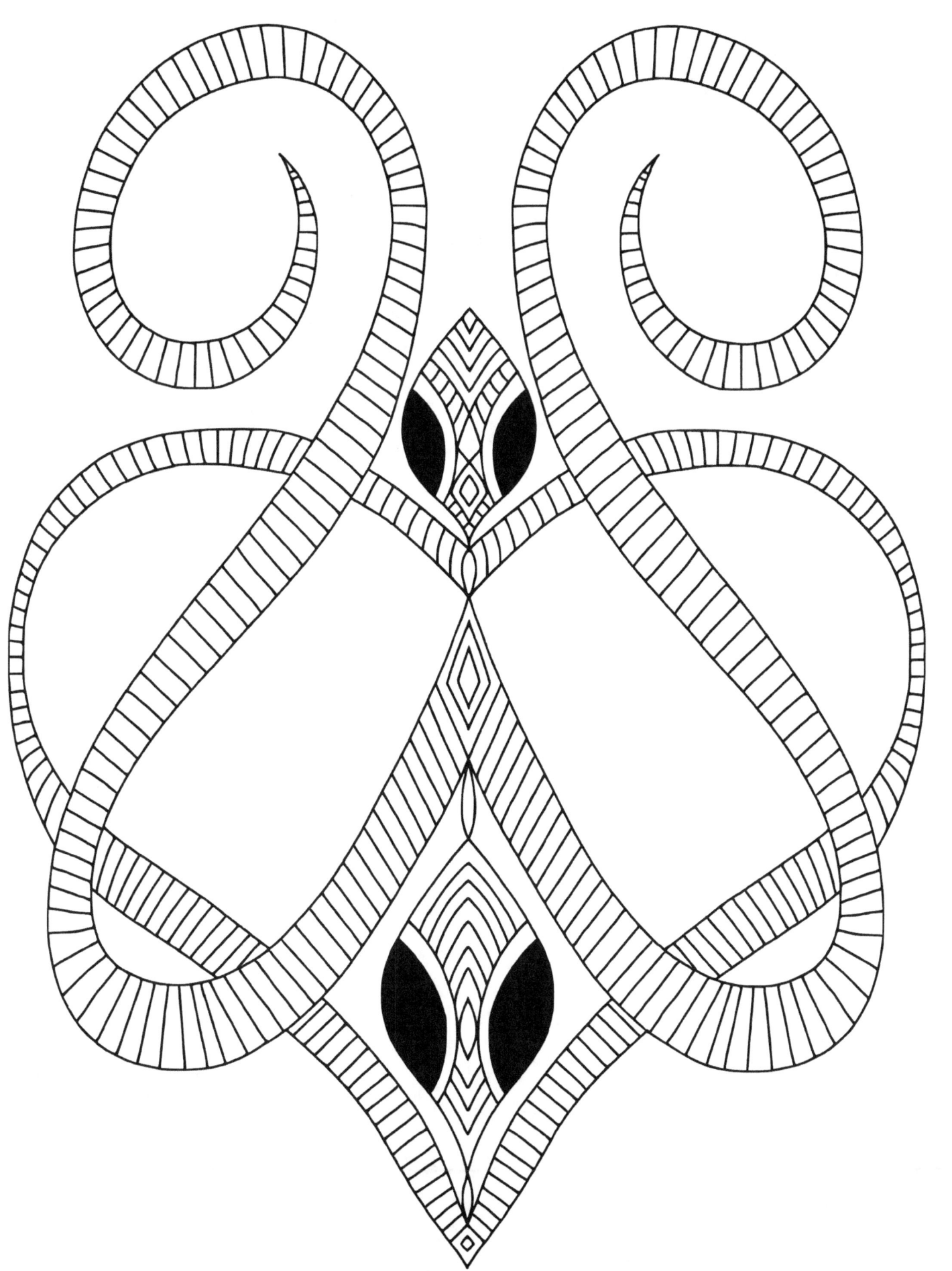

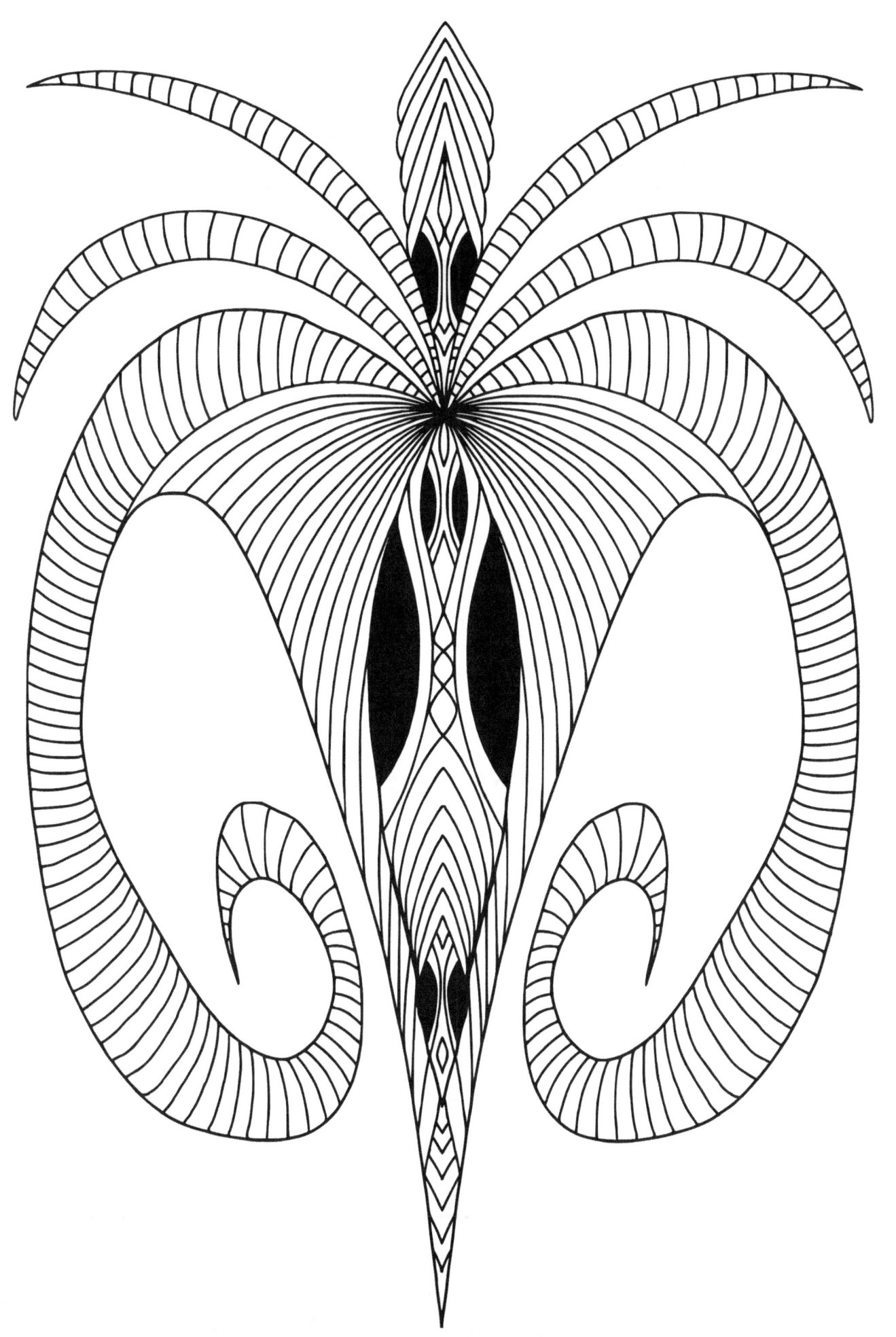

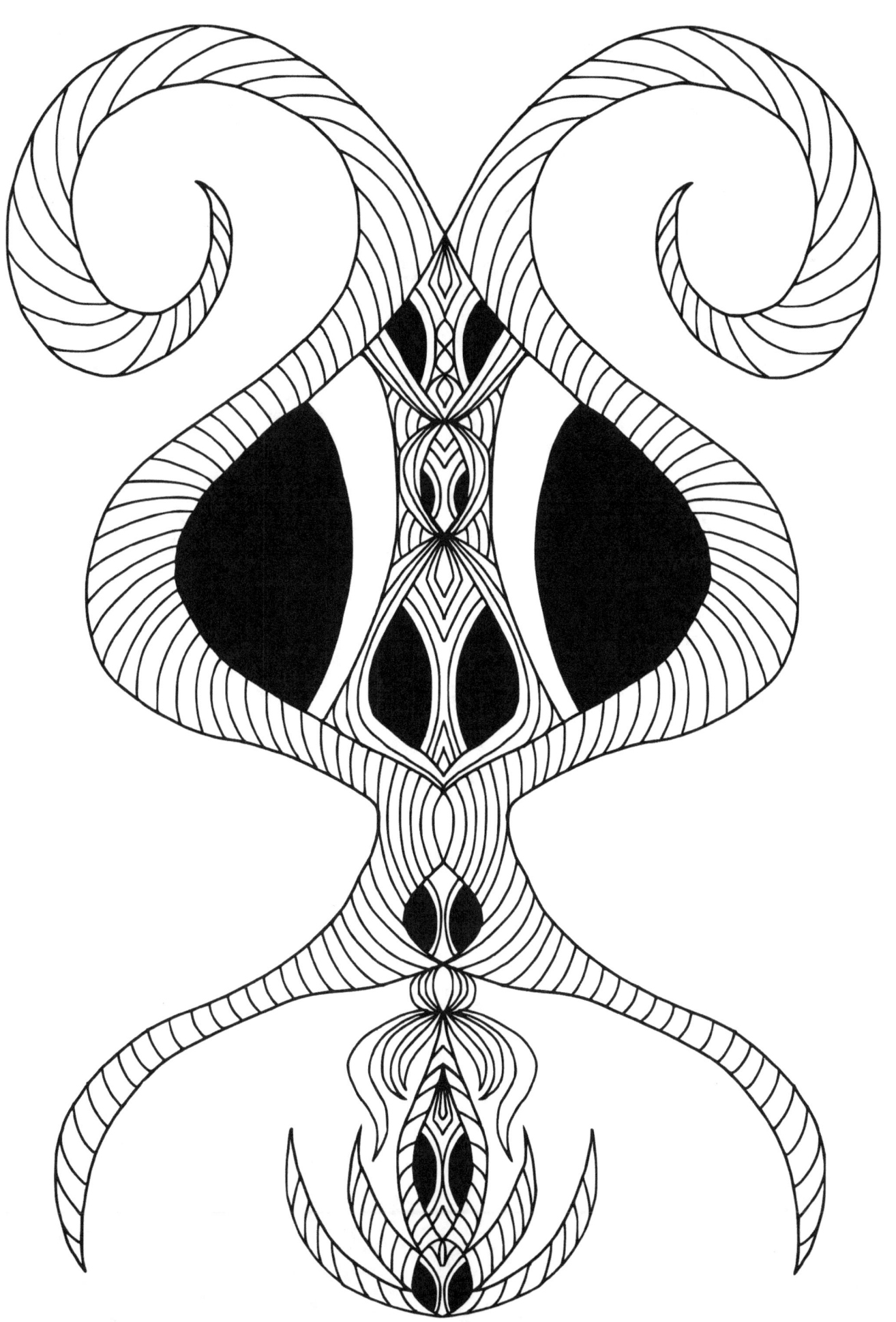

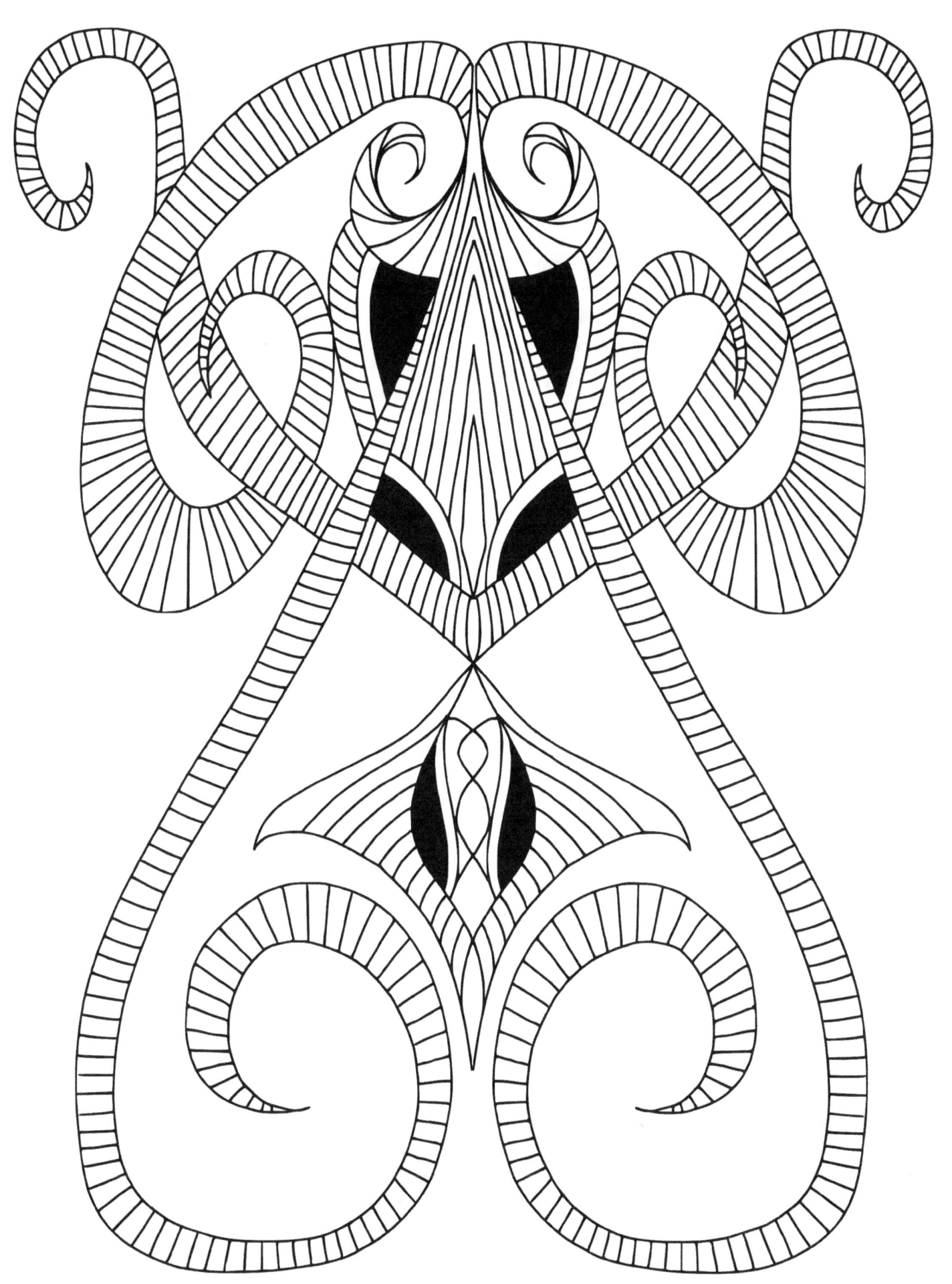

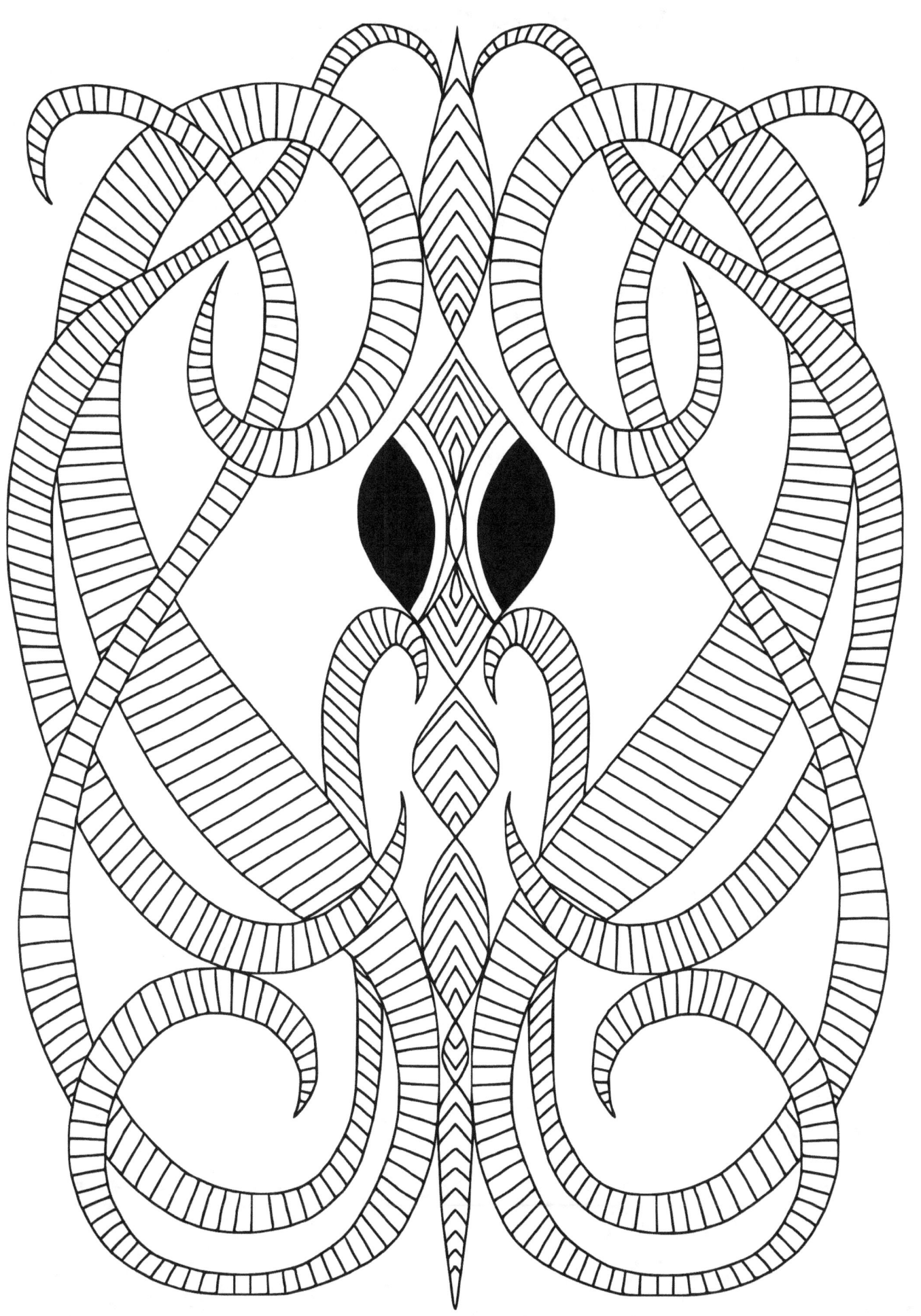

Bonus Upside Down versions......

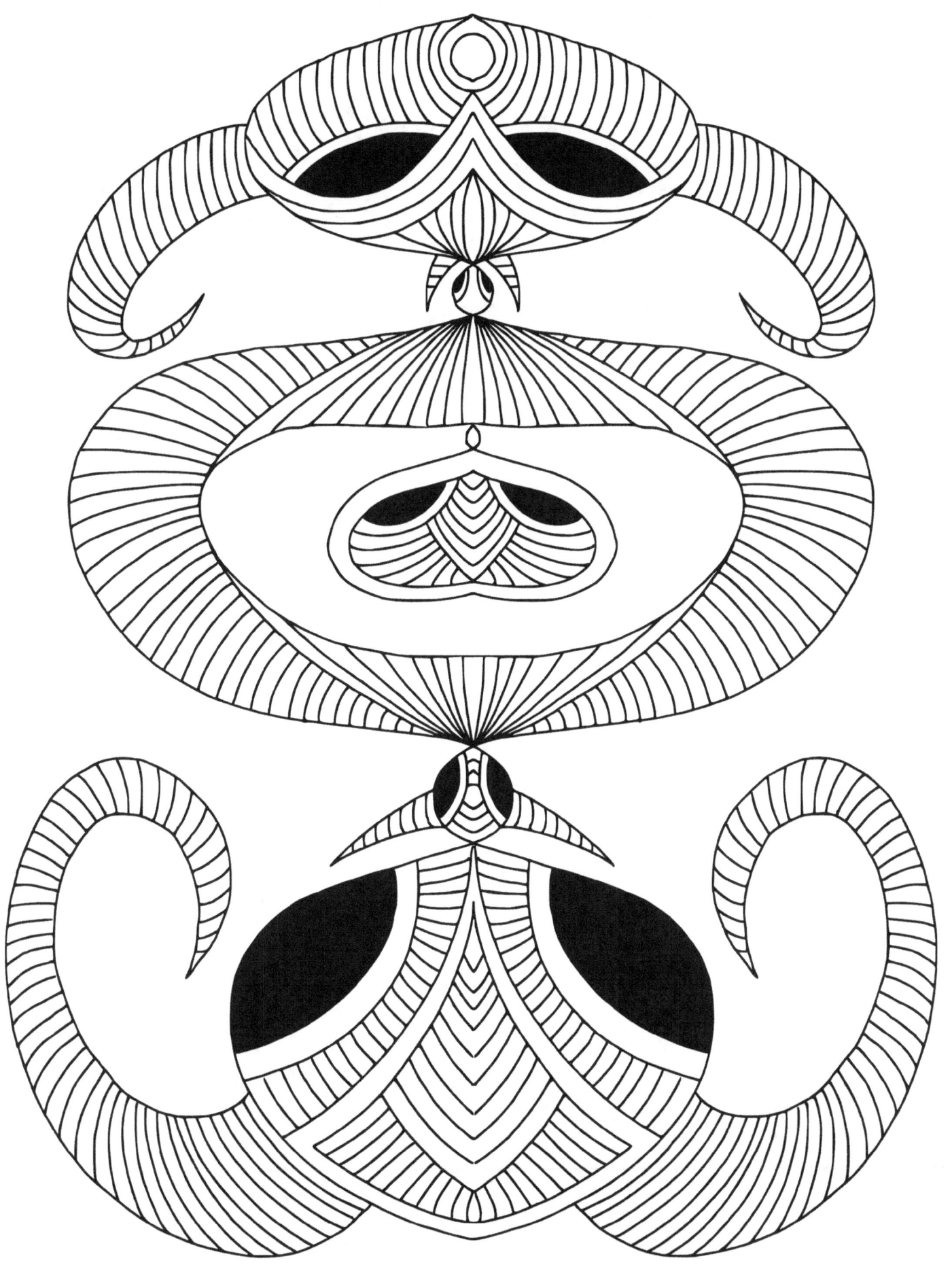

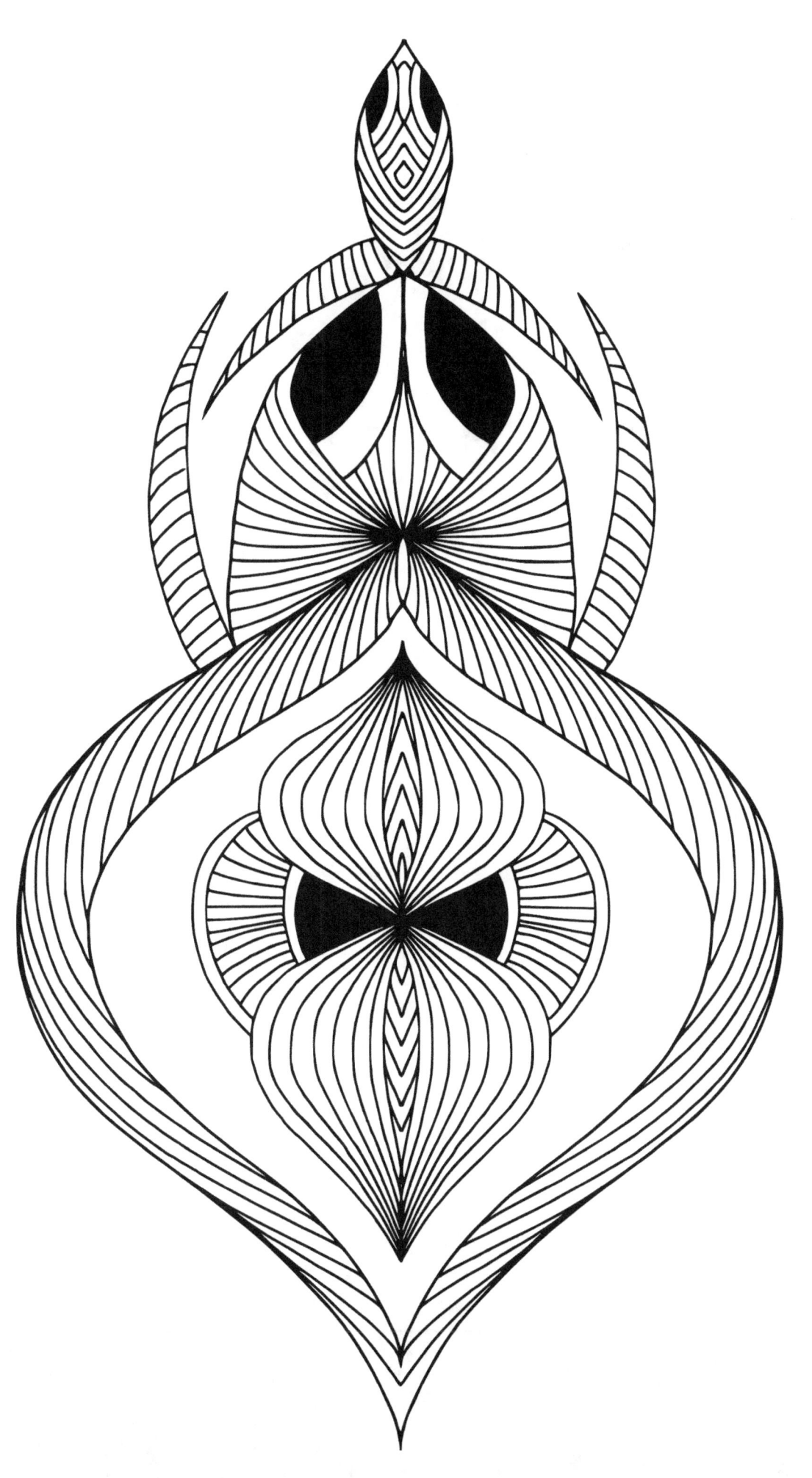

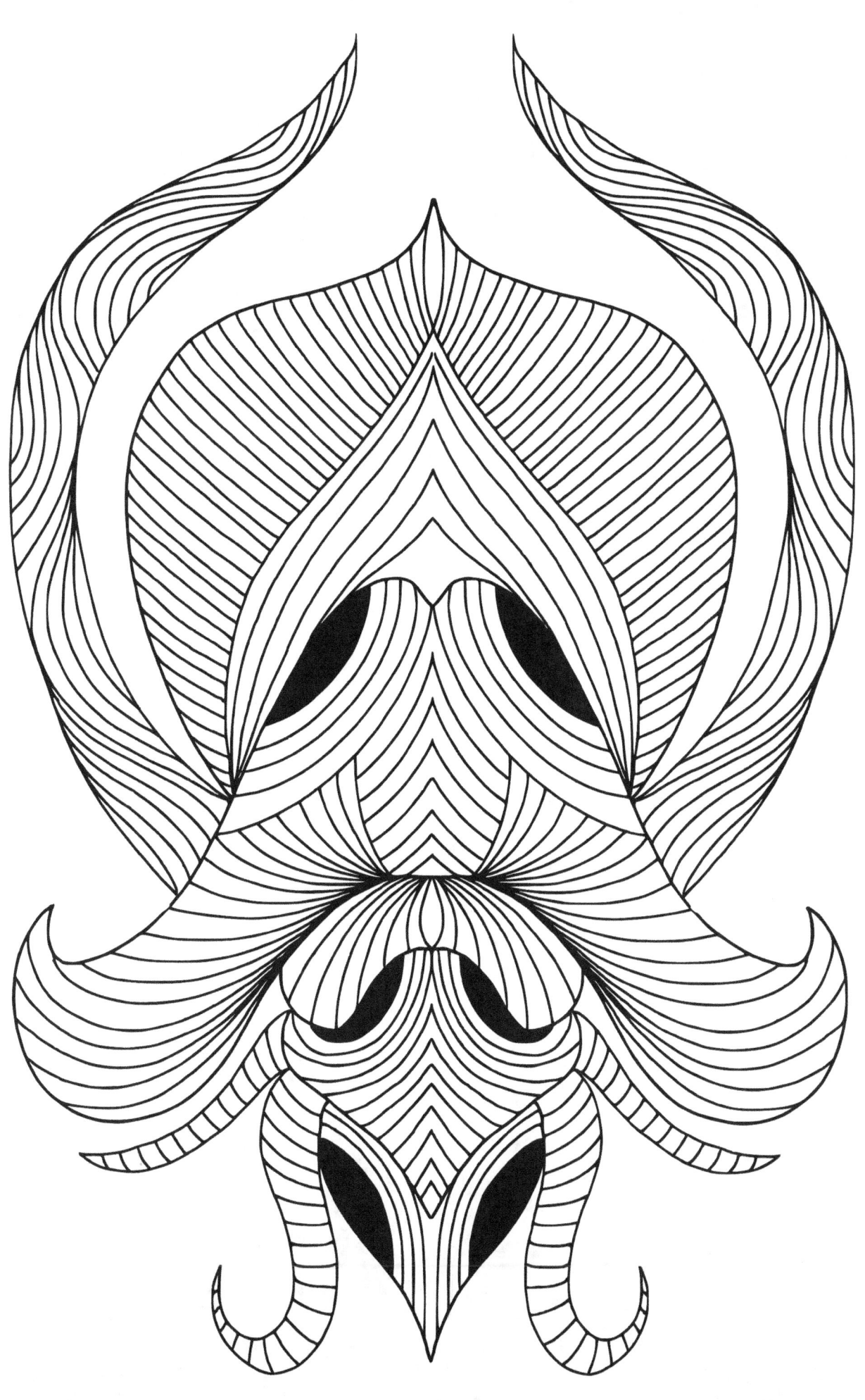

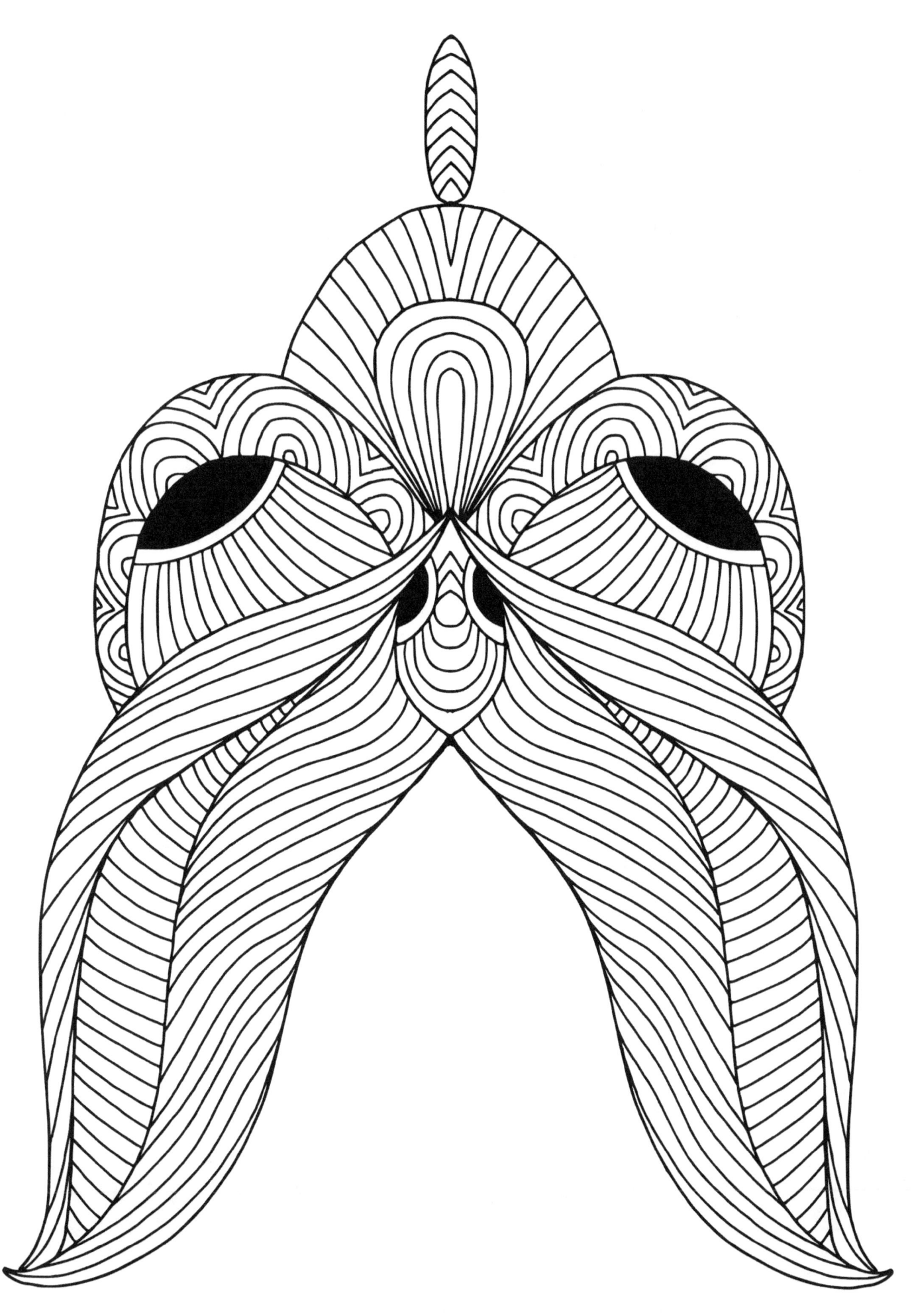

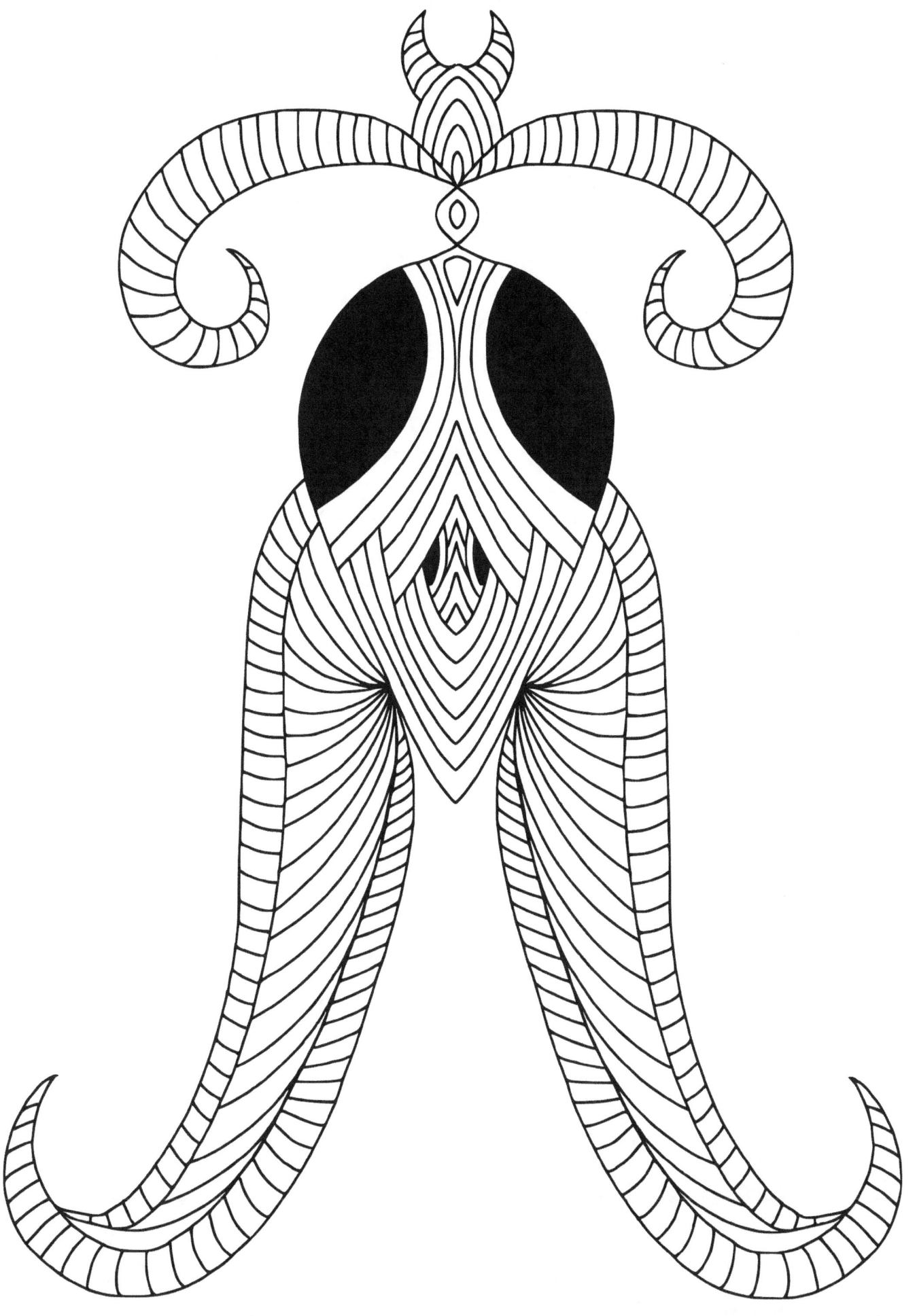

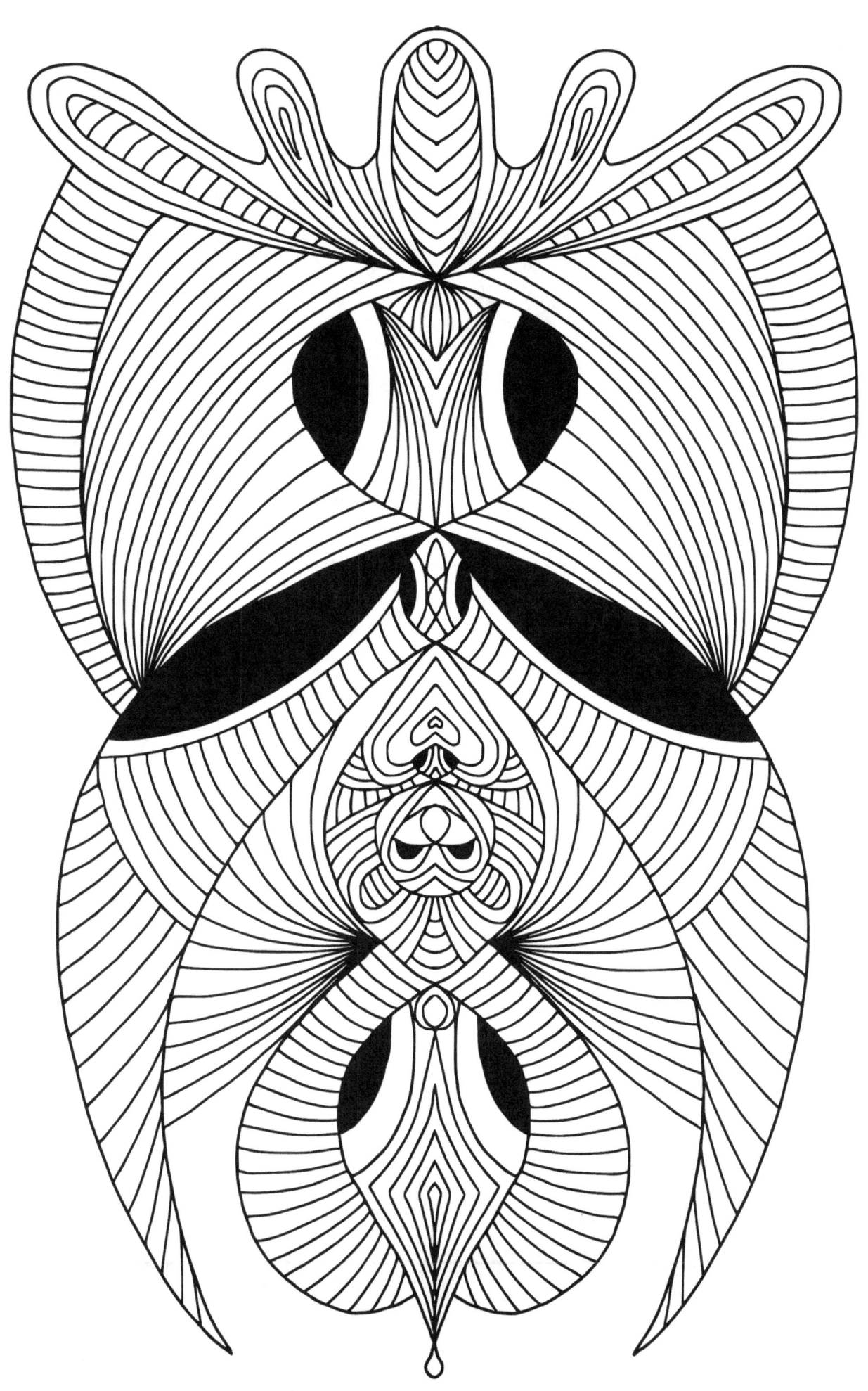

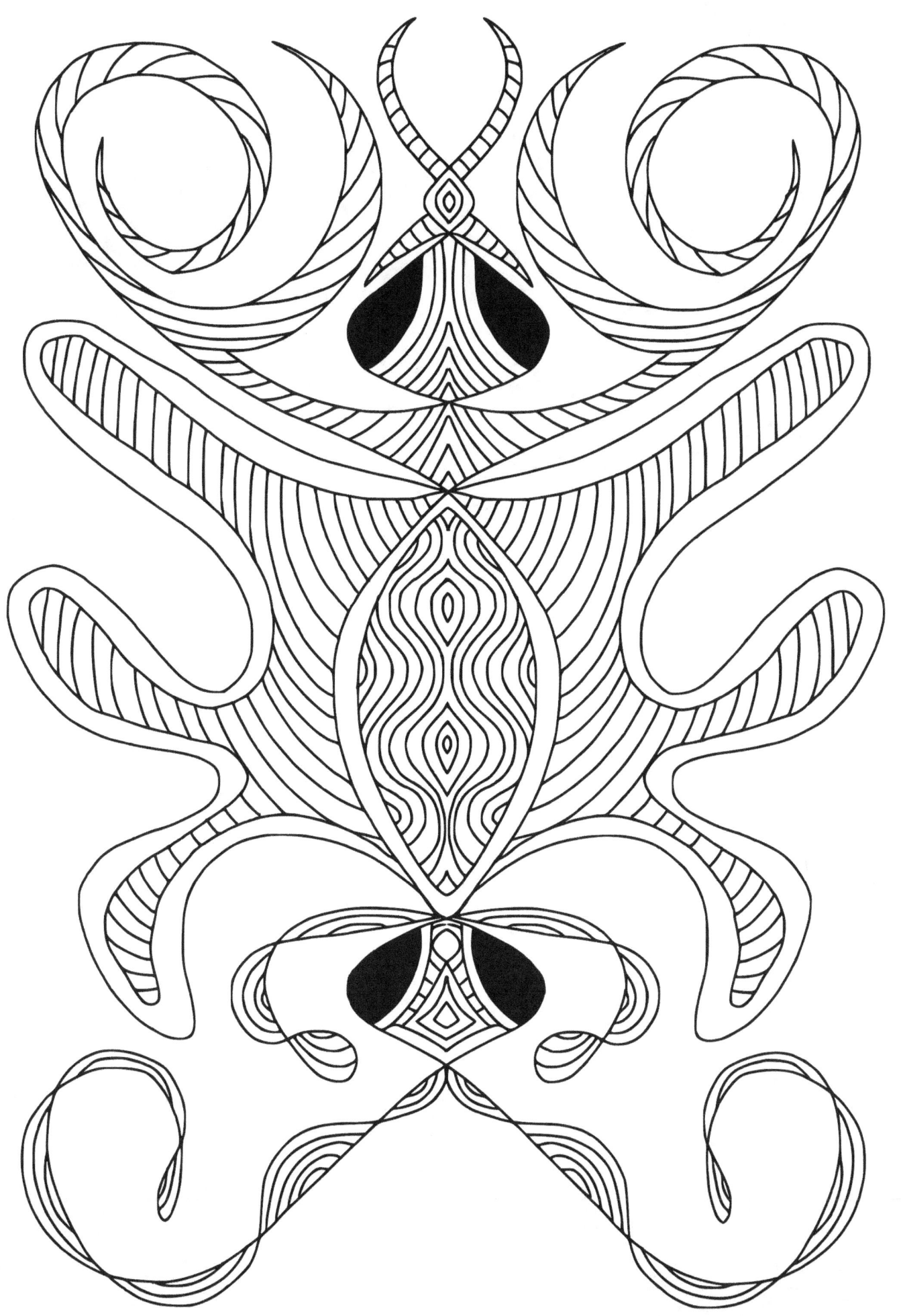

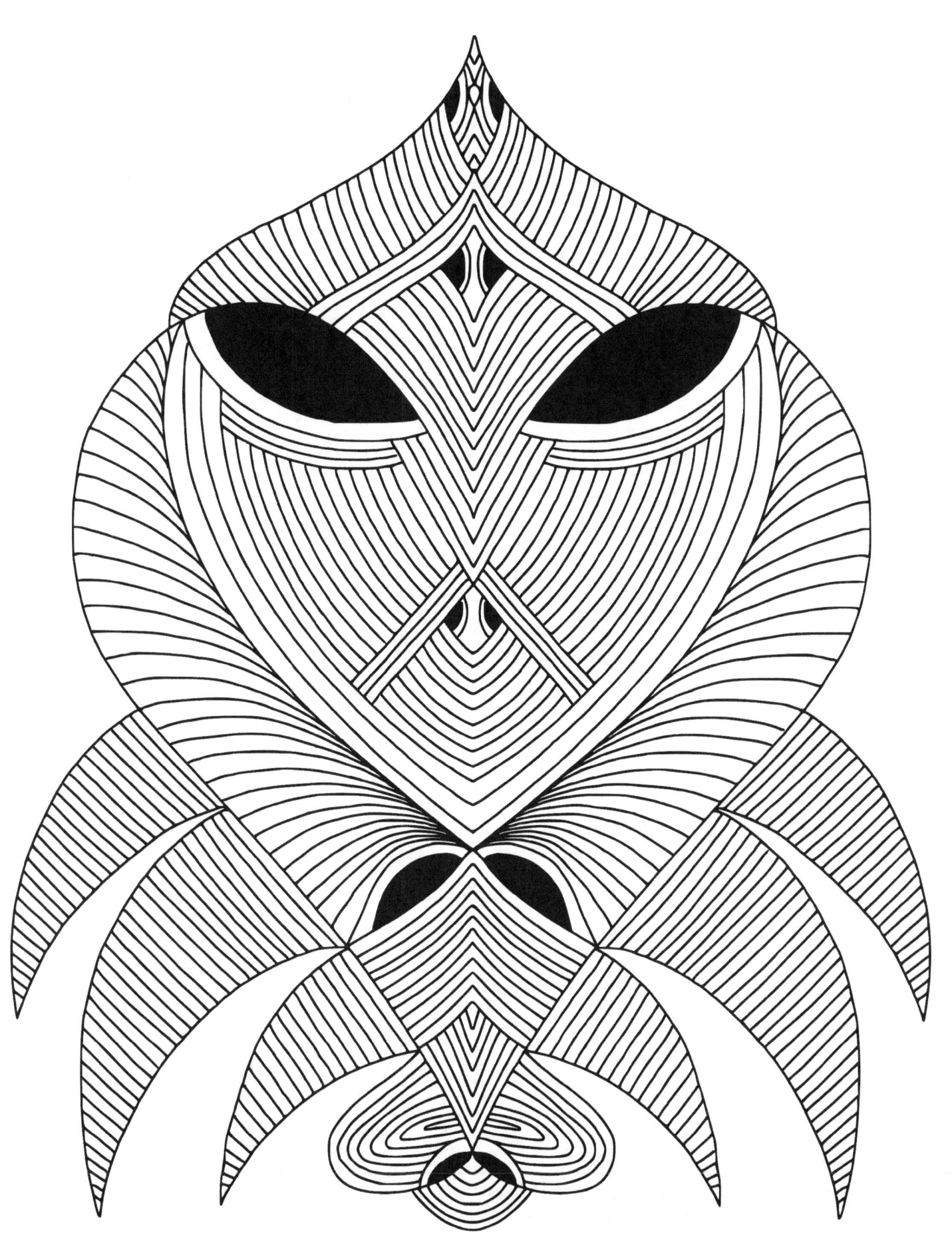

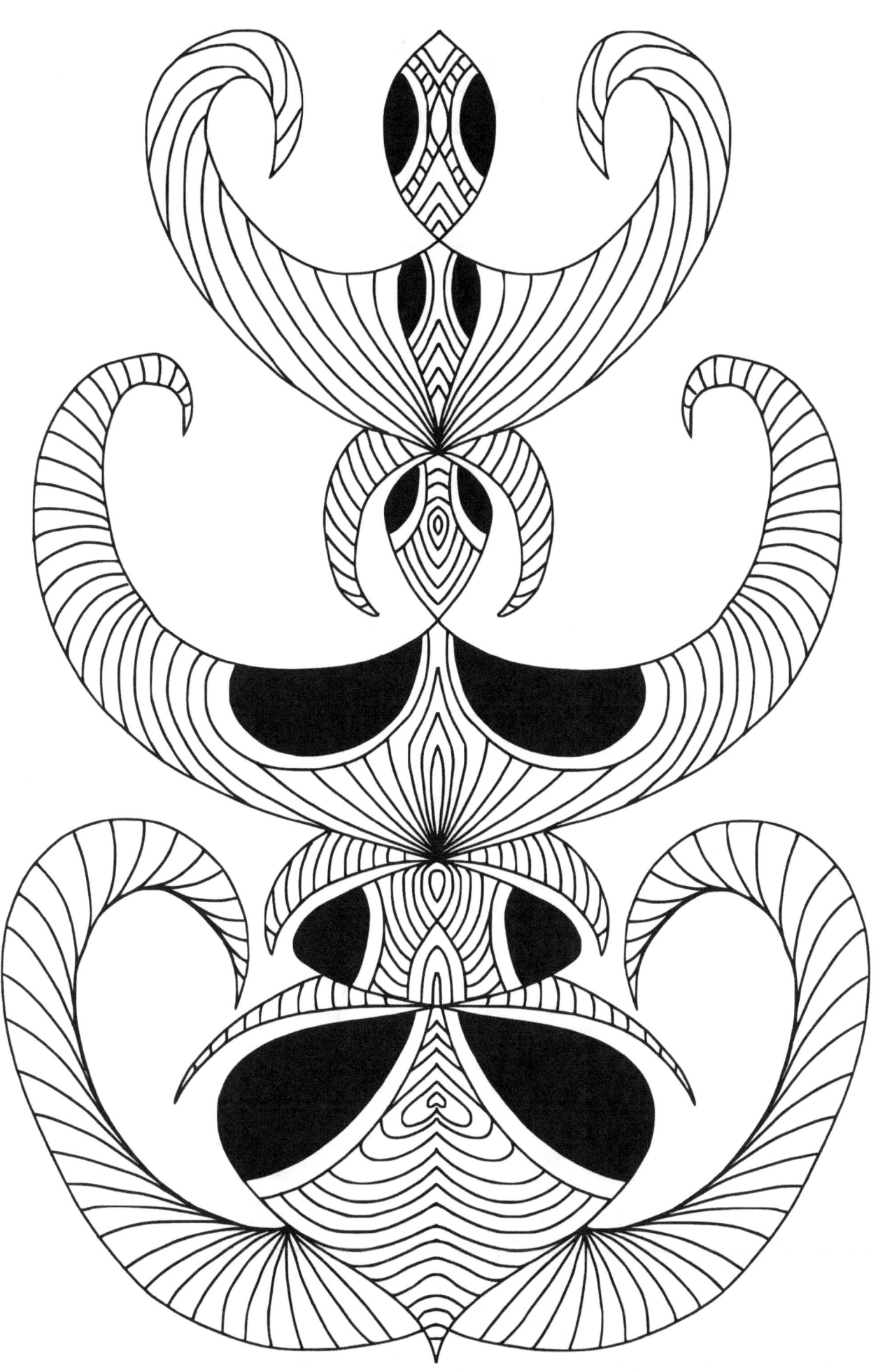

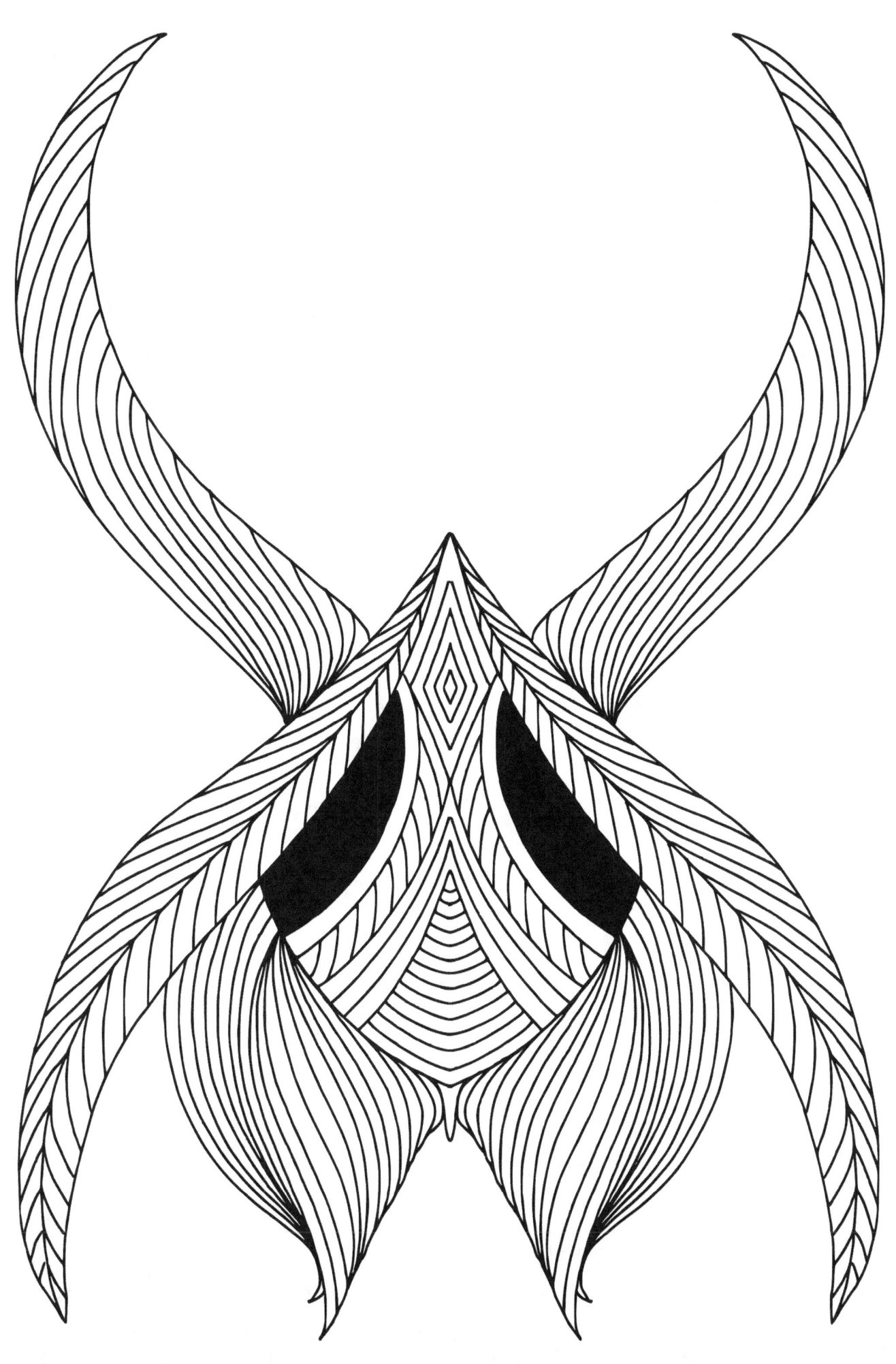

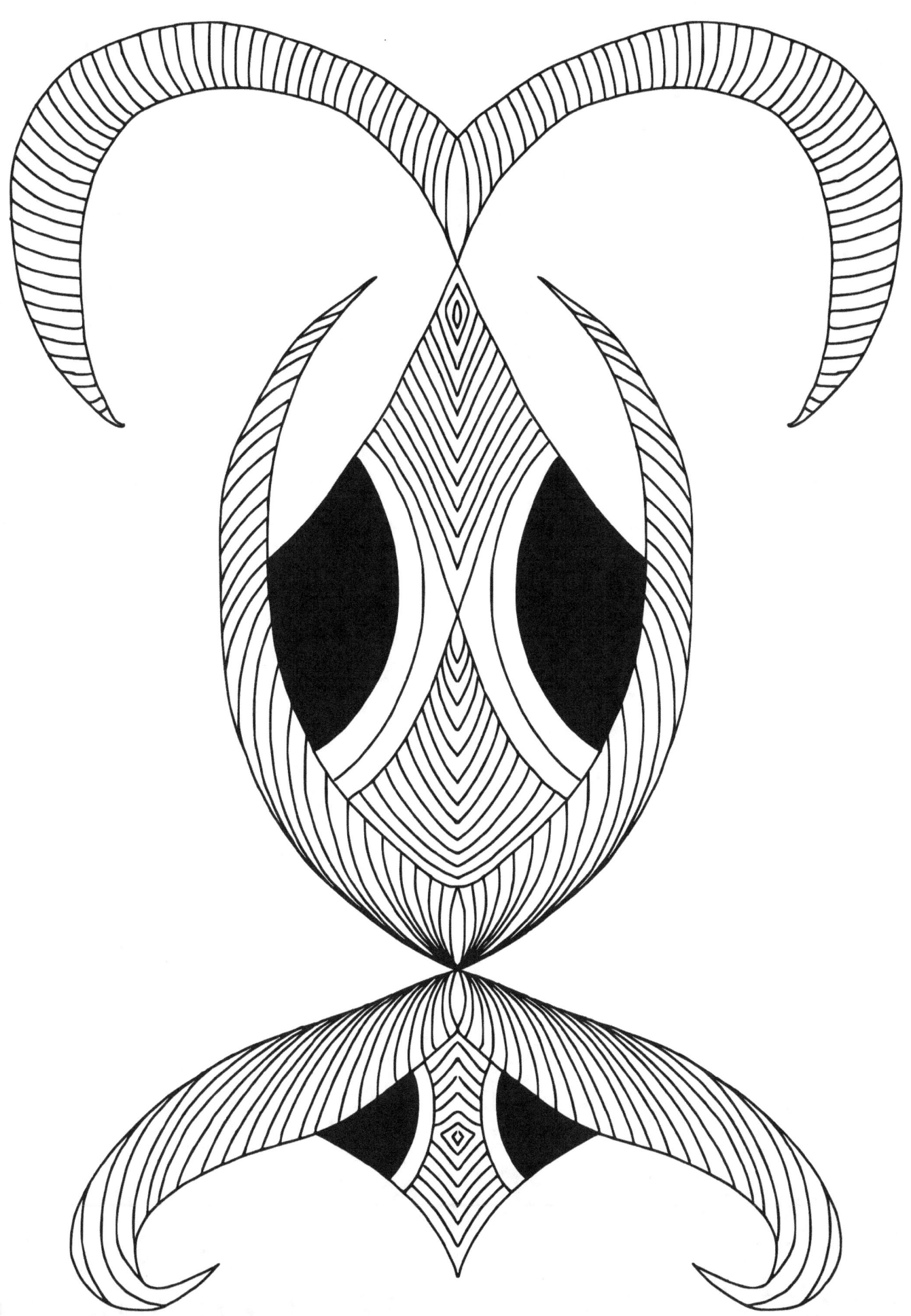

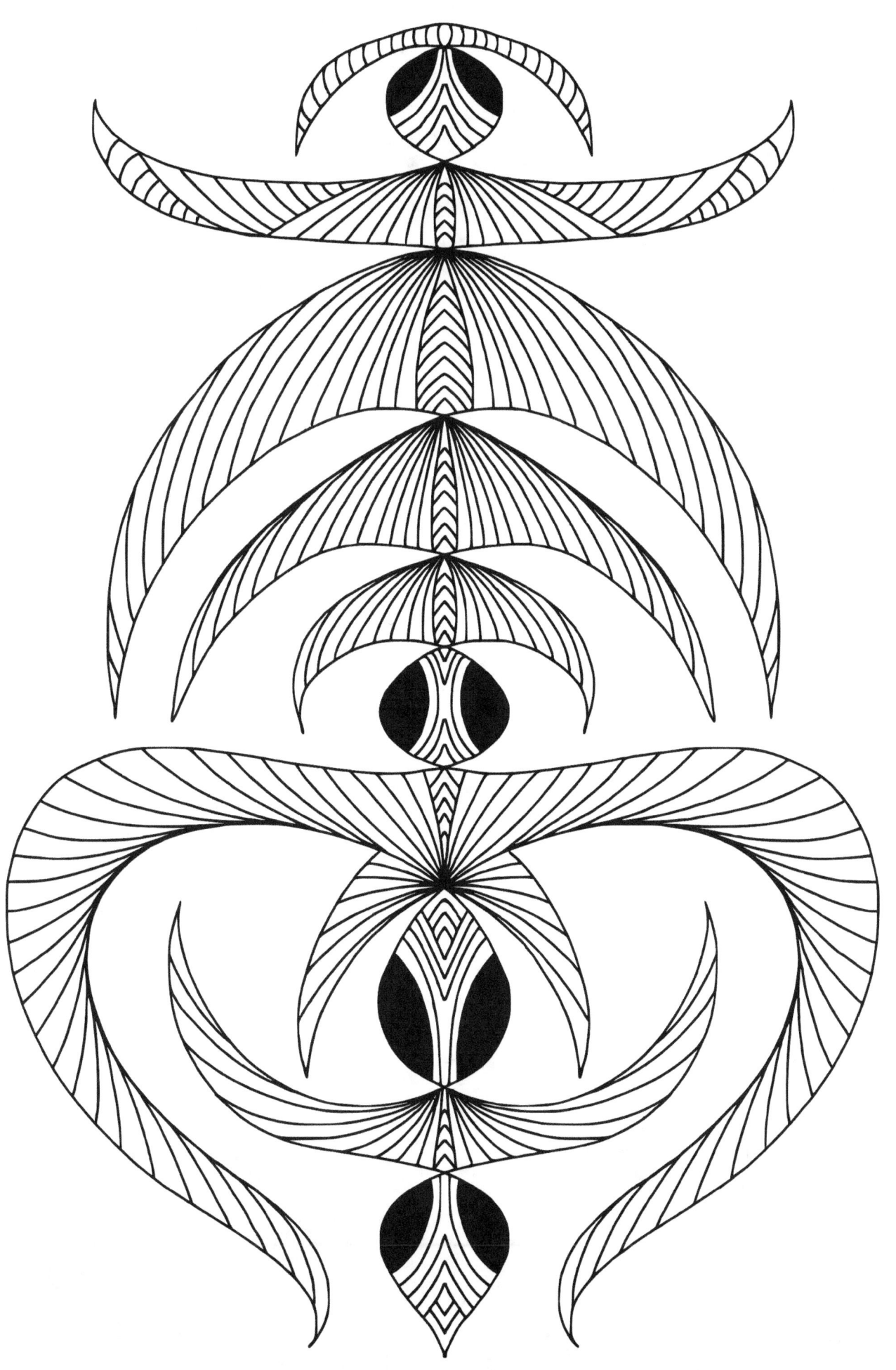

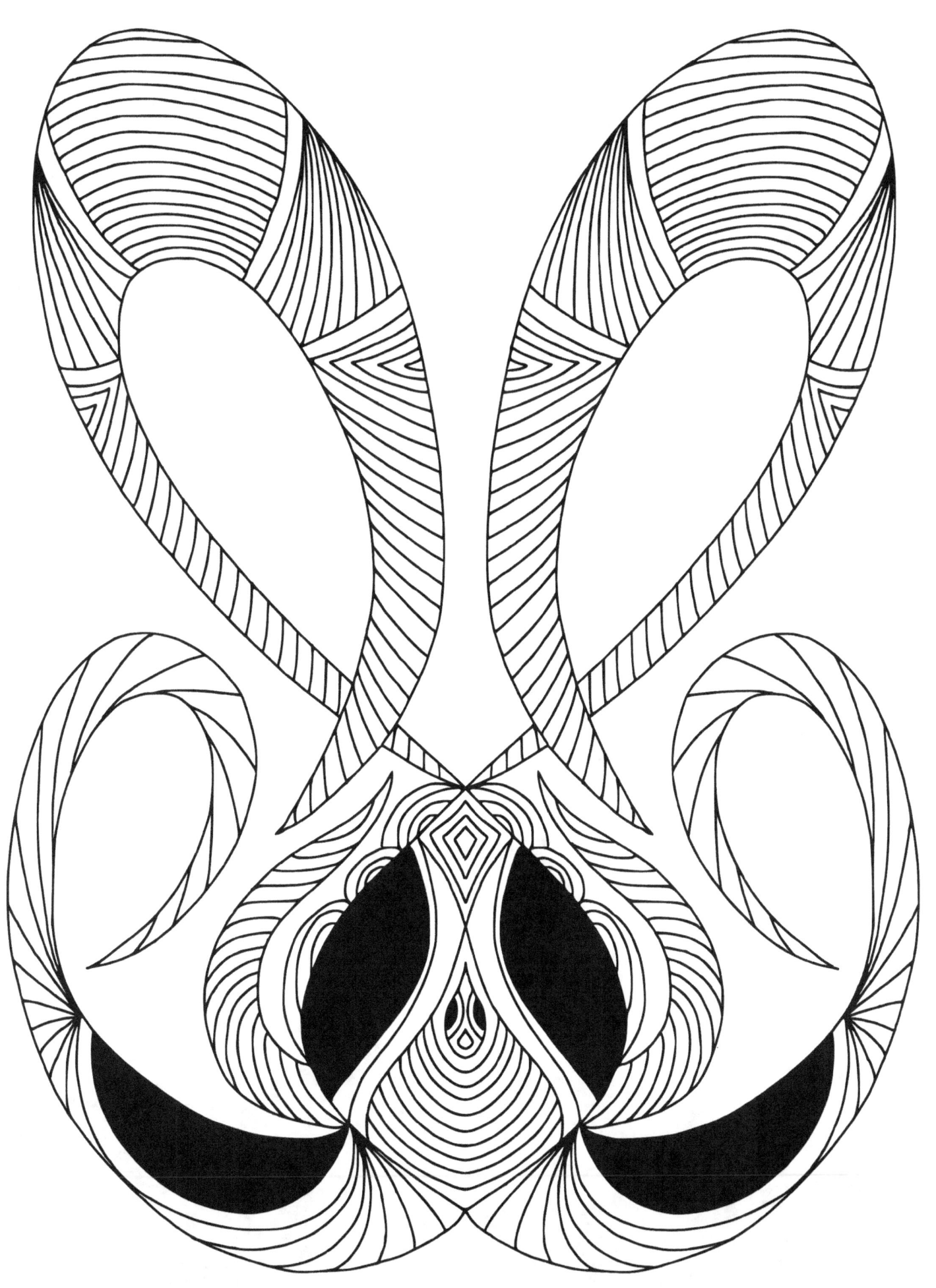

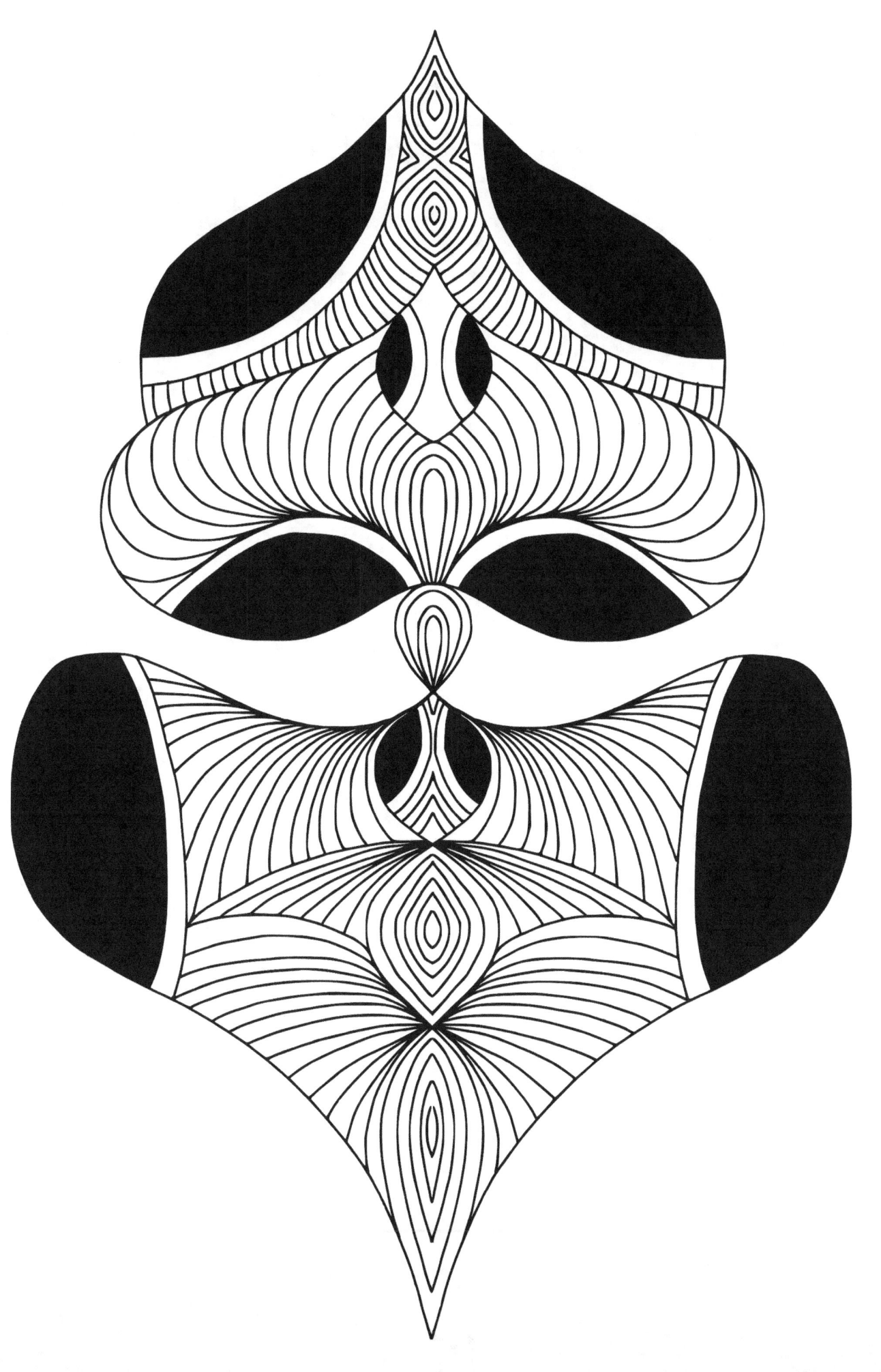

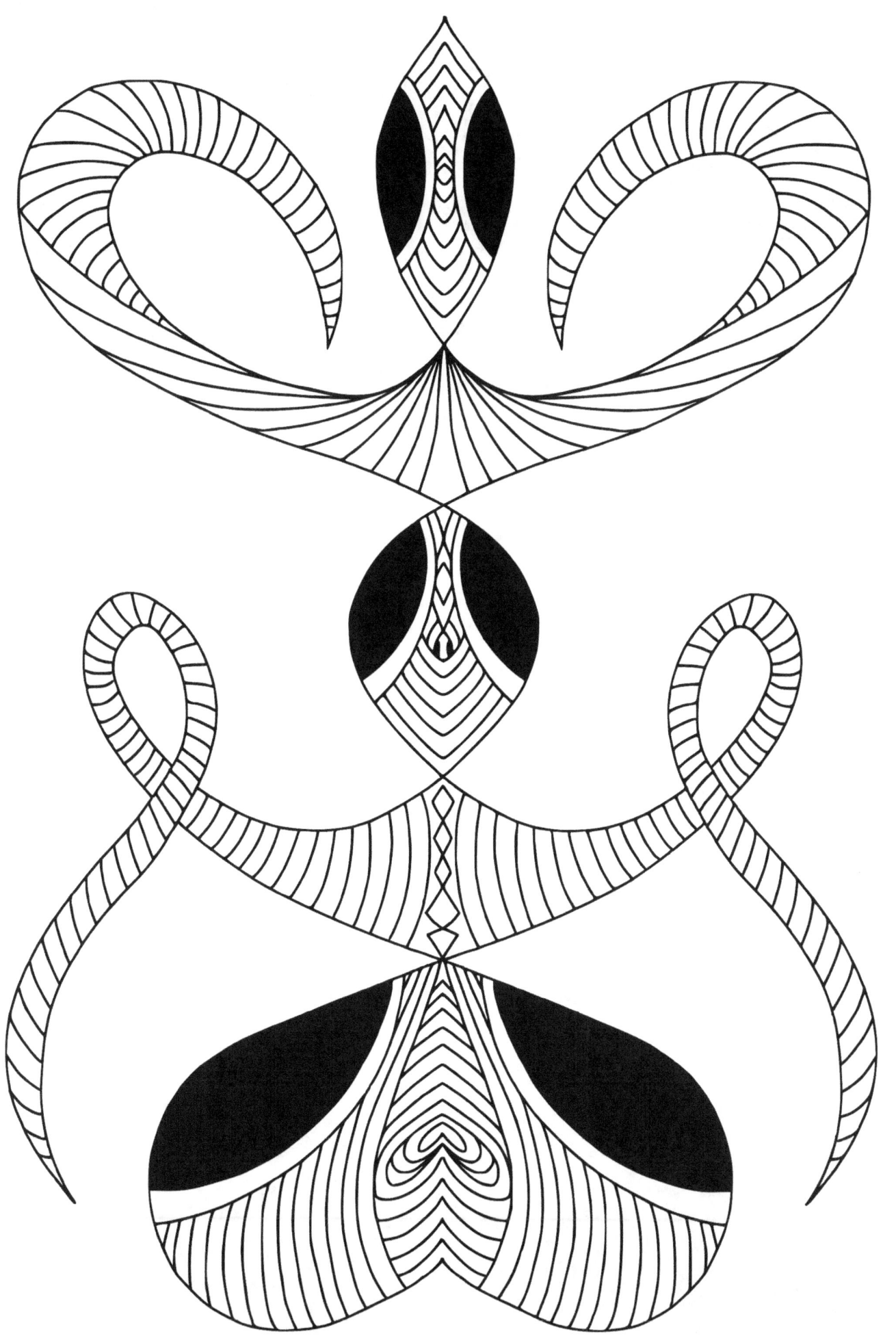

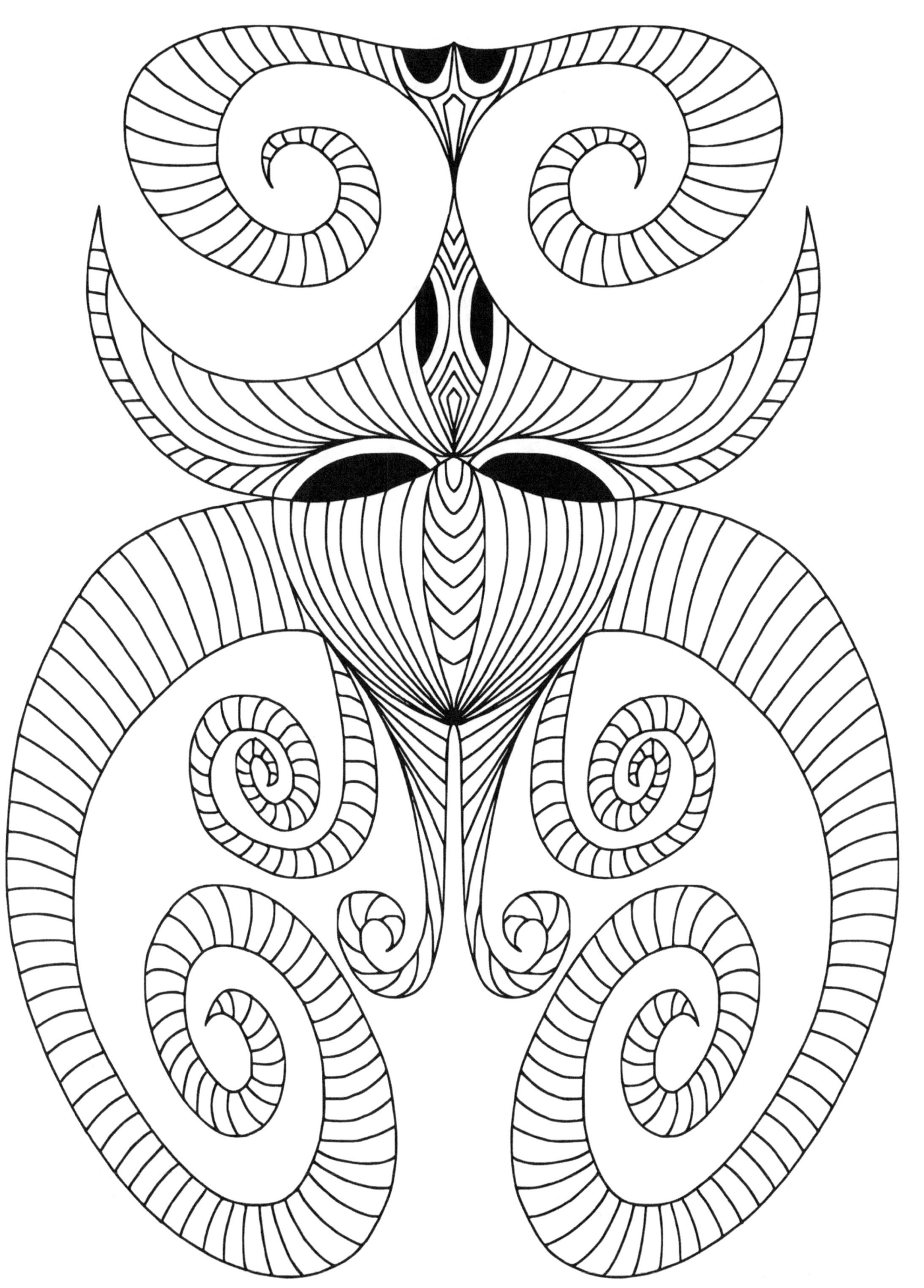

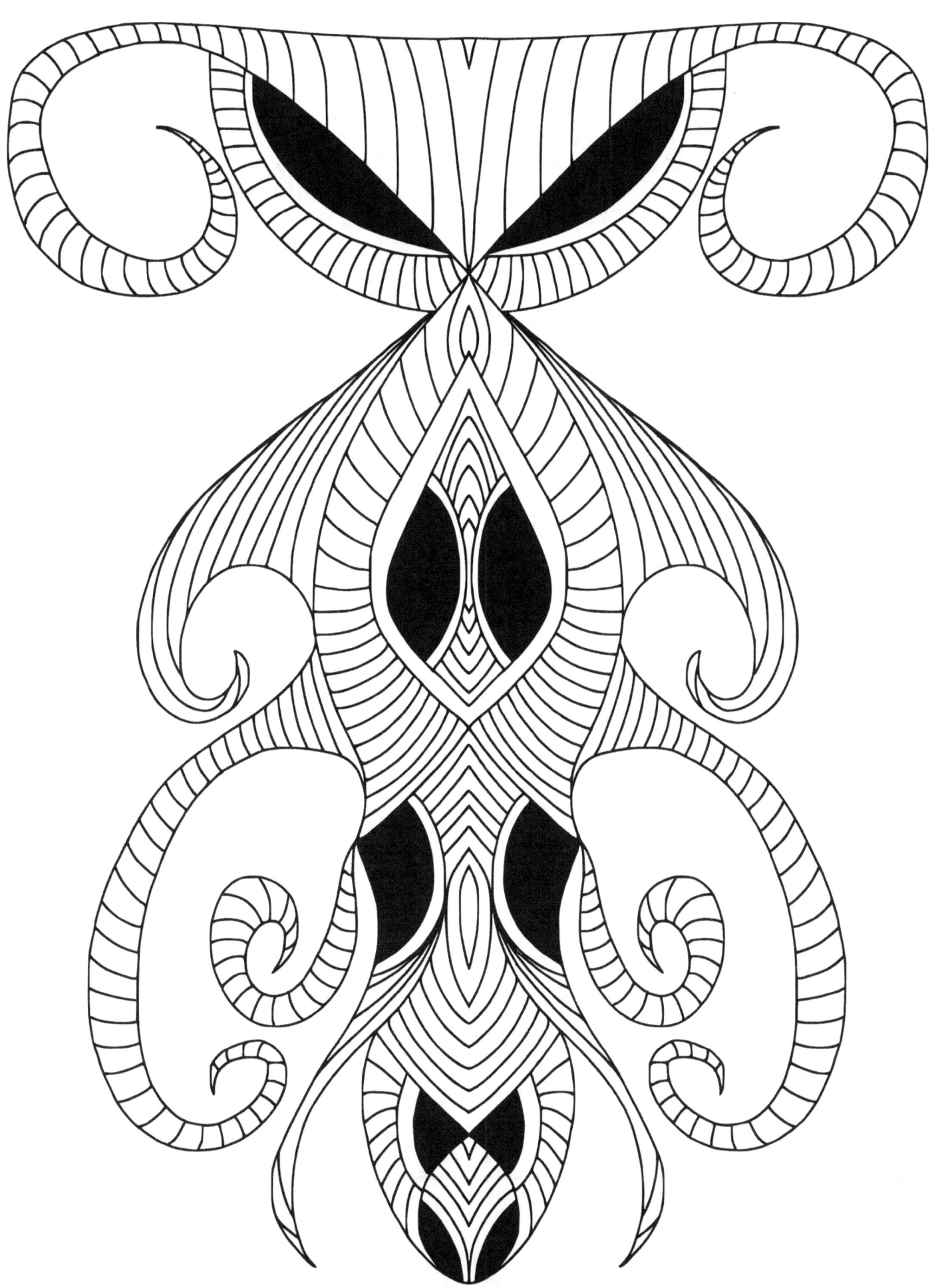

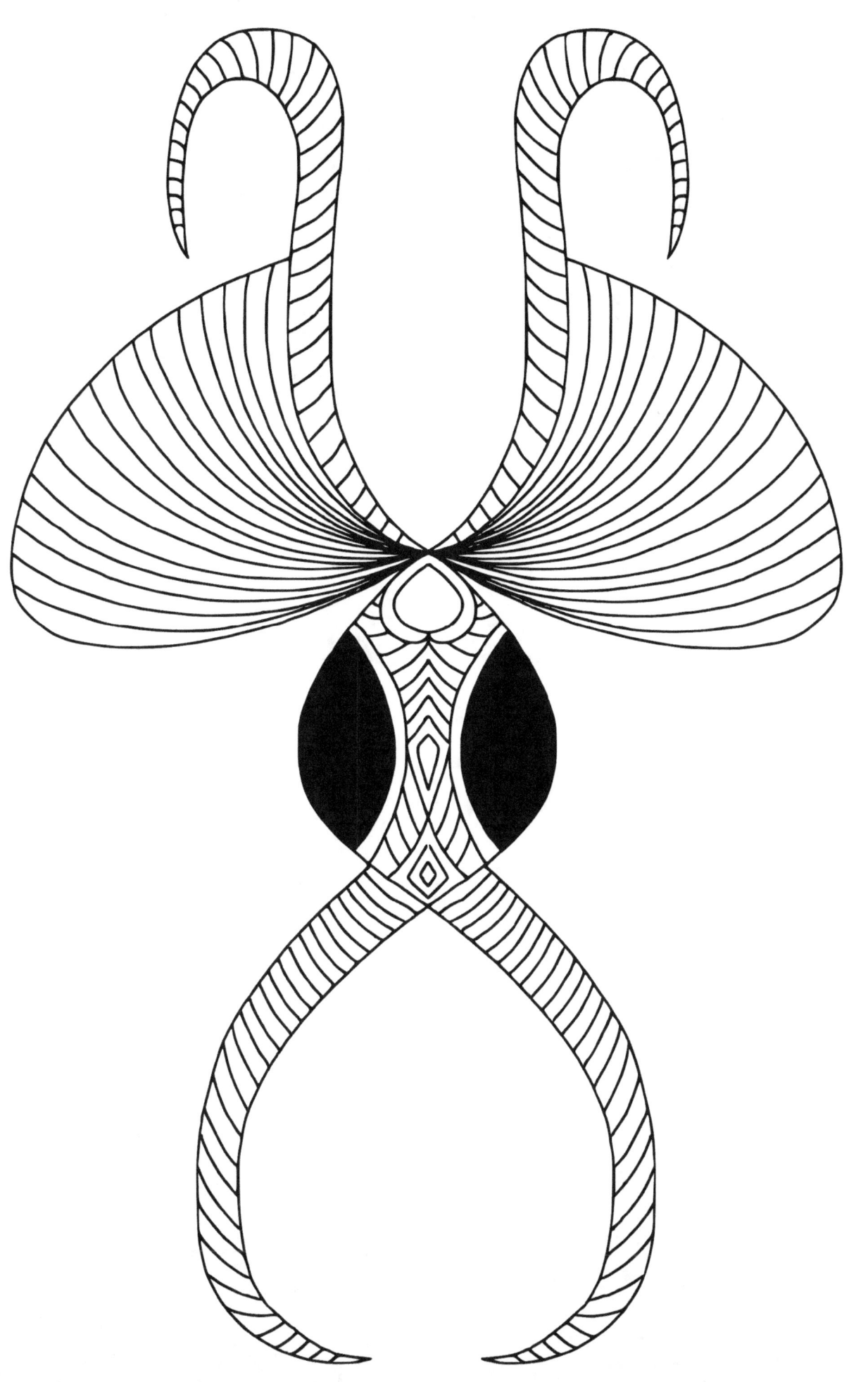

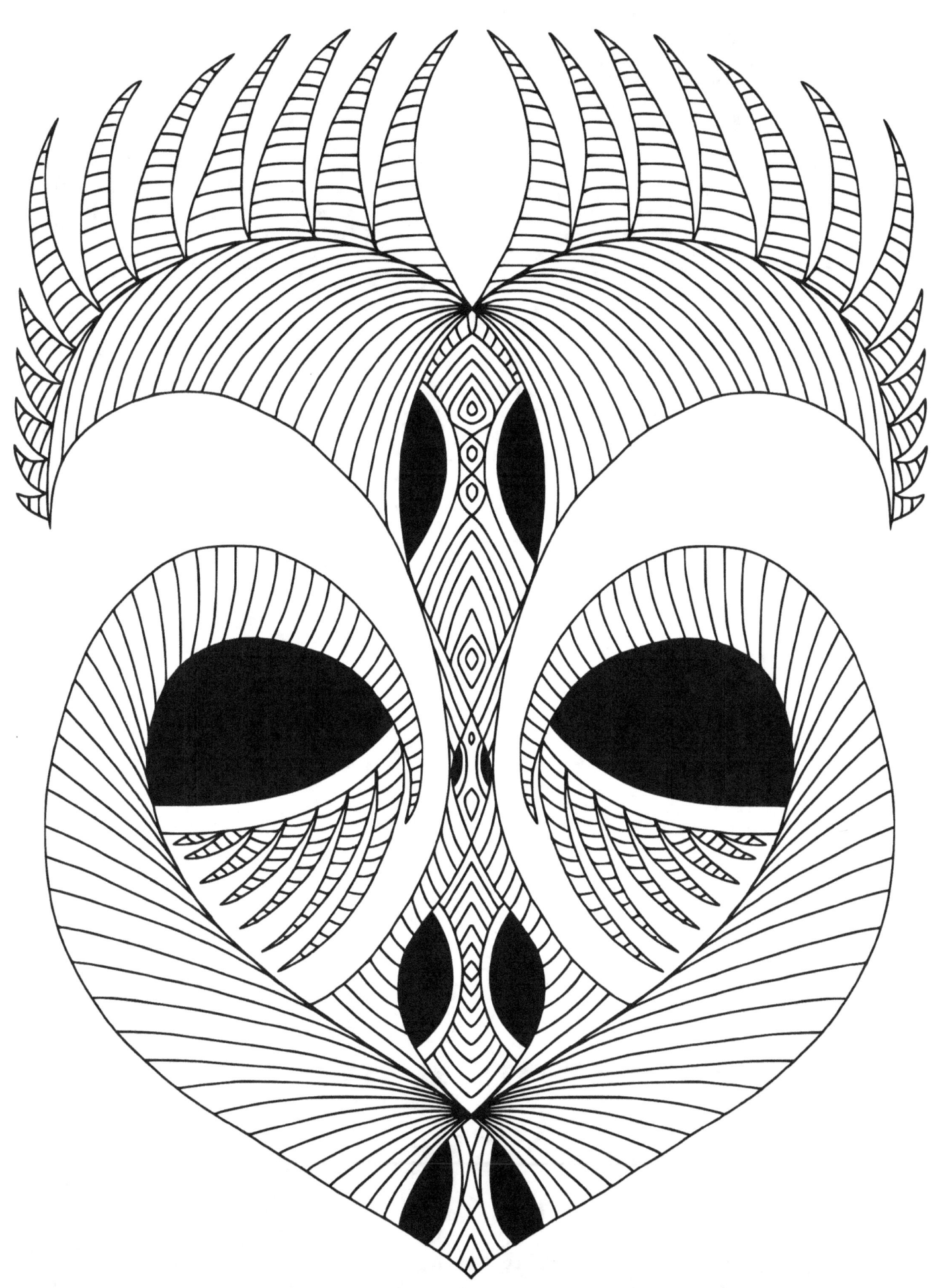

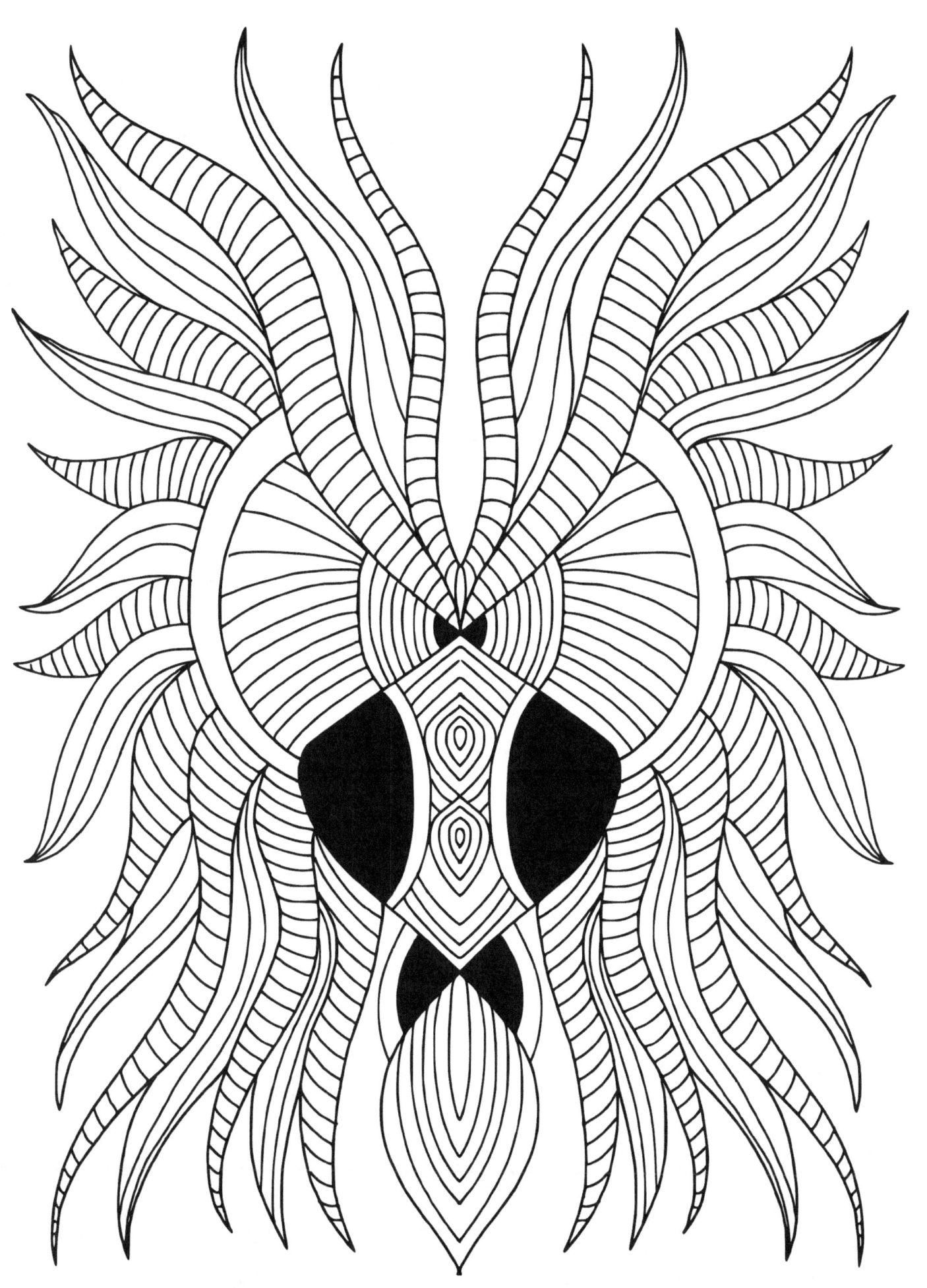

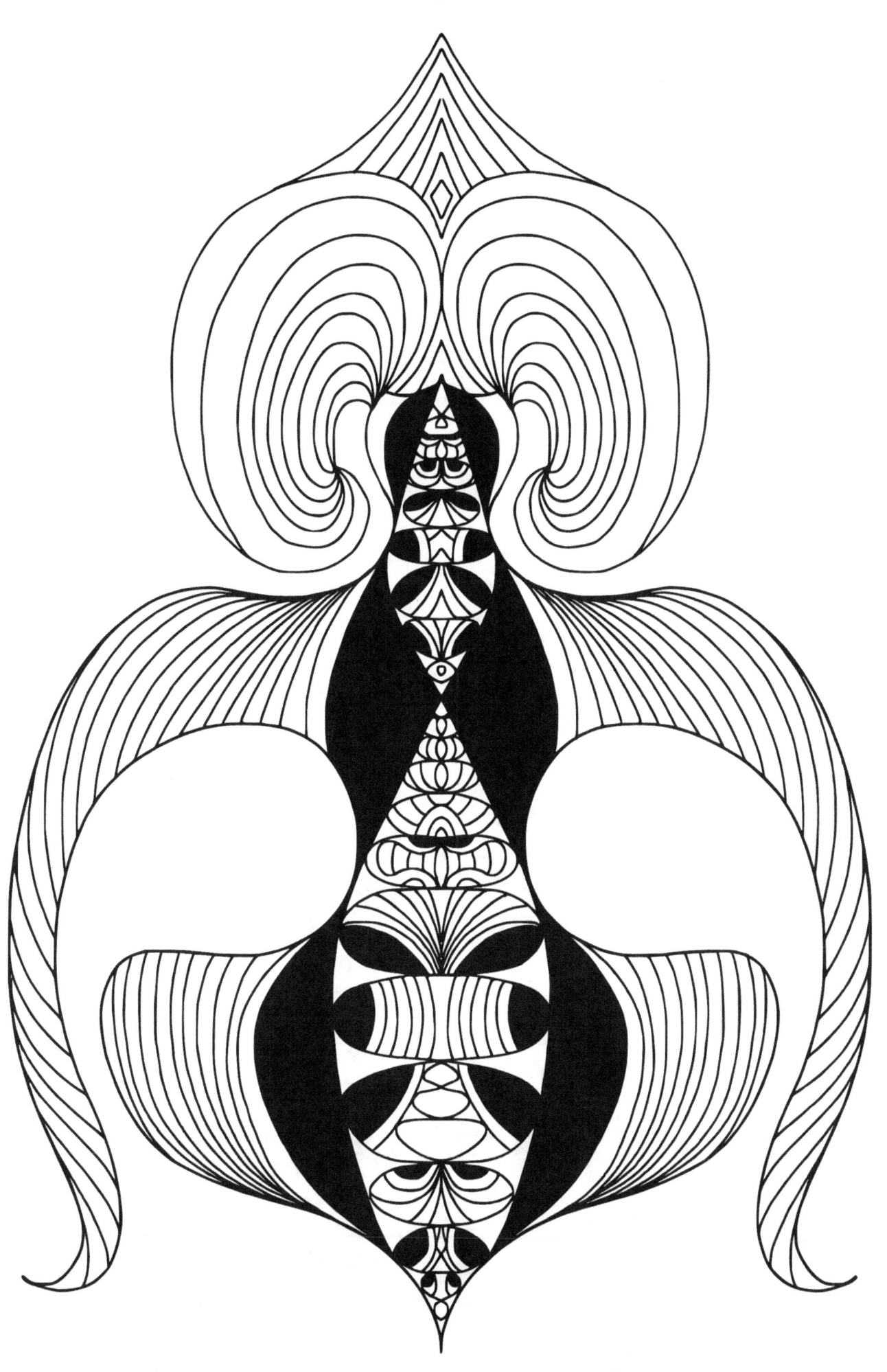

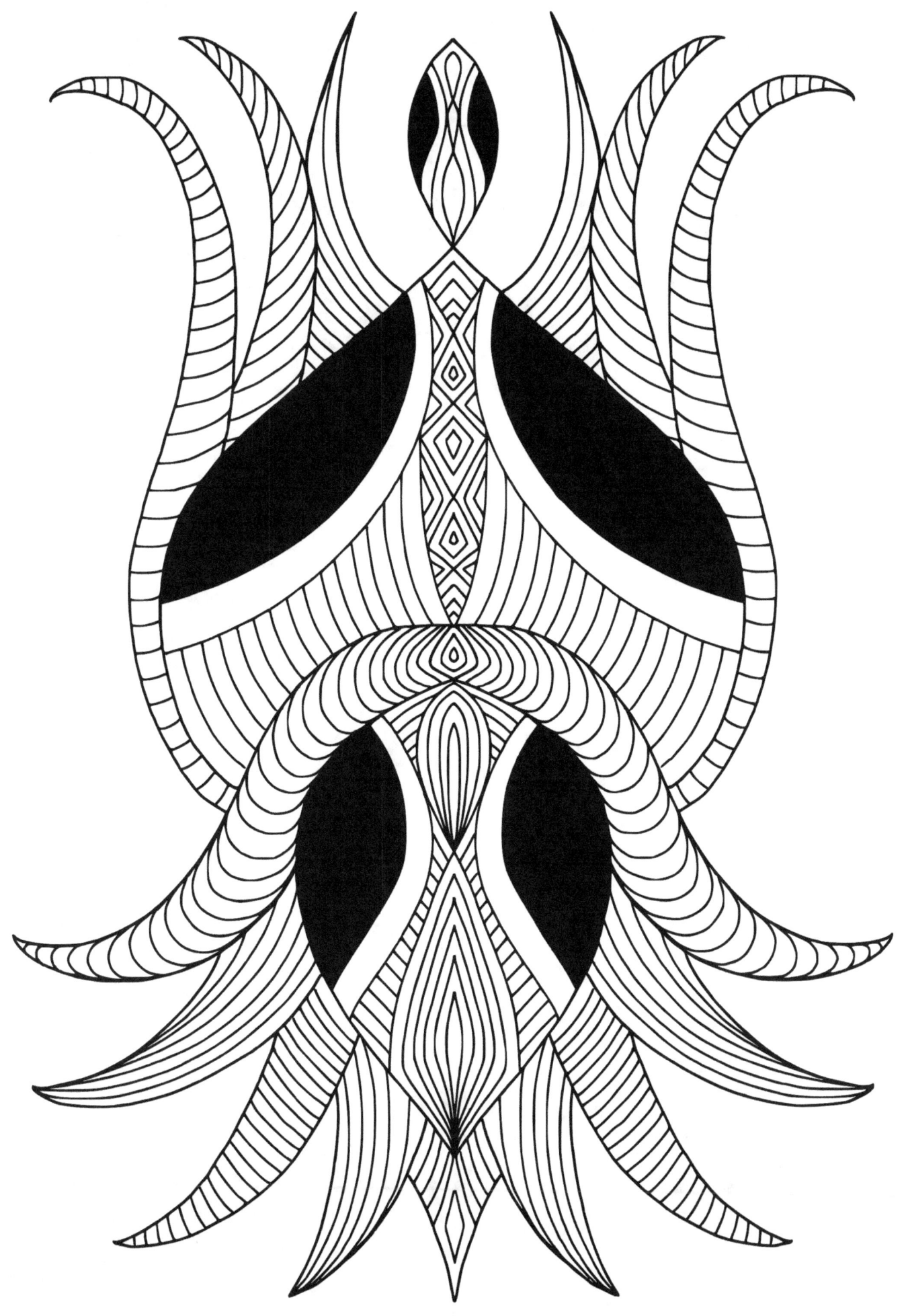

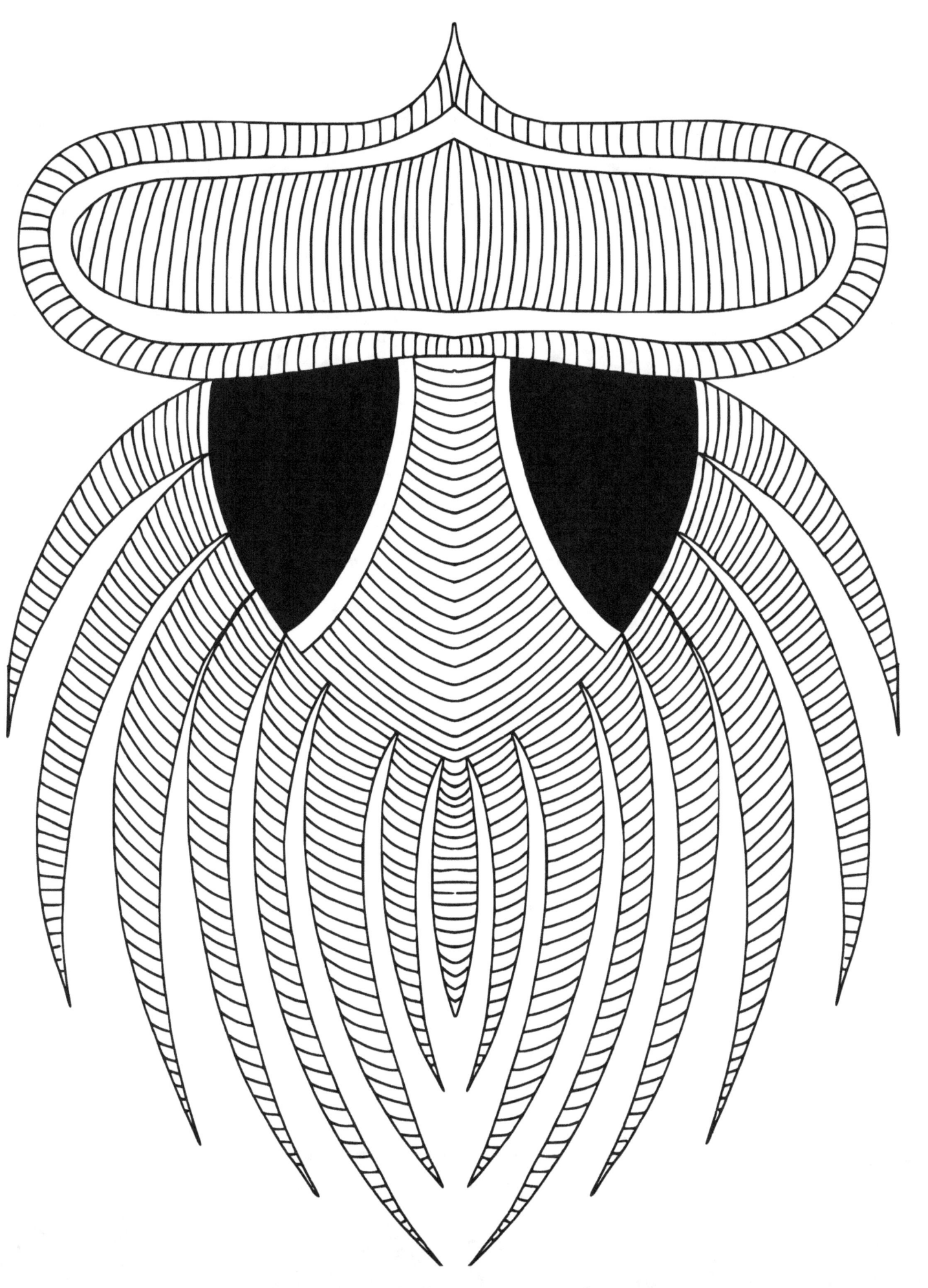

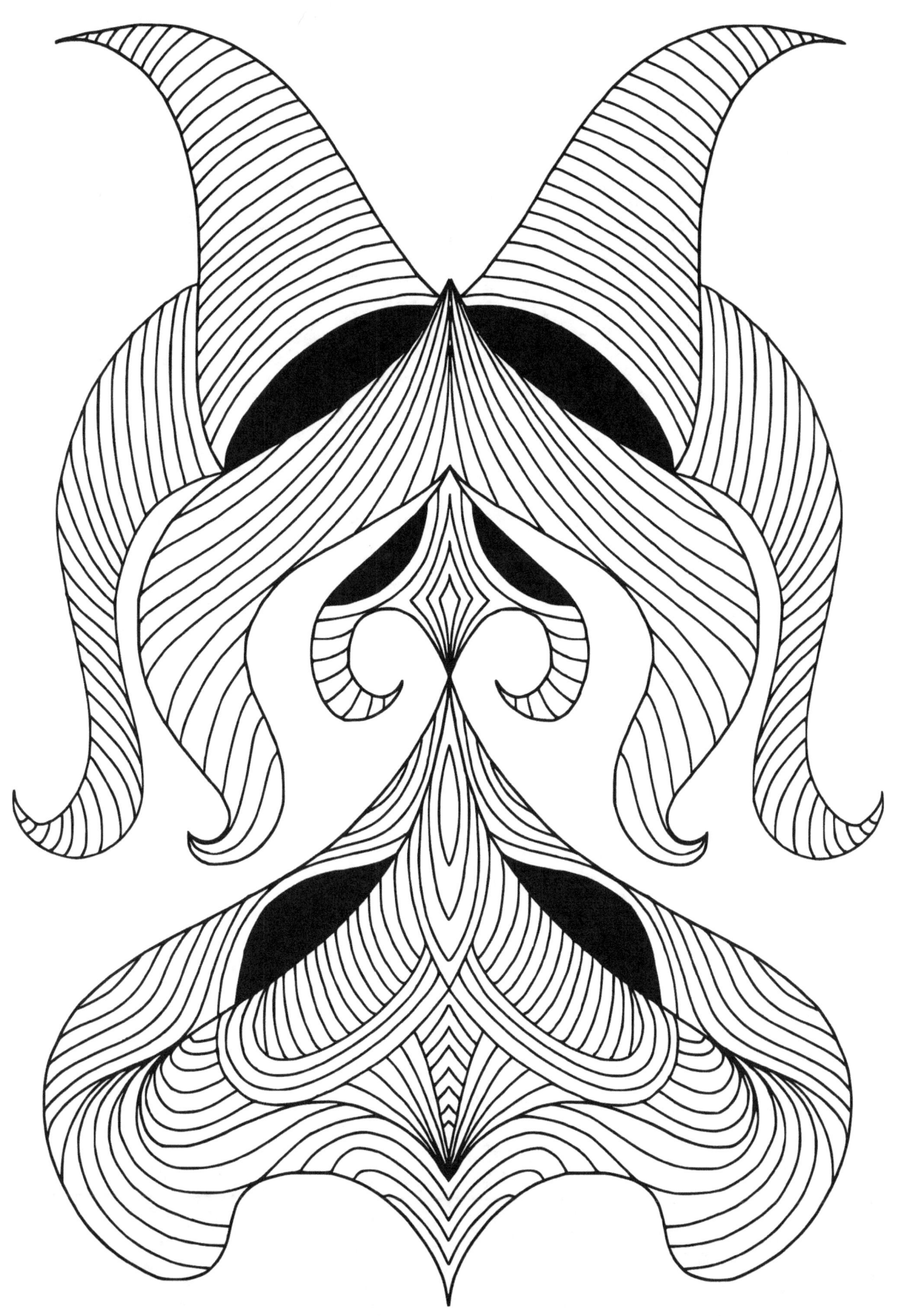

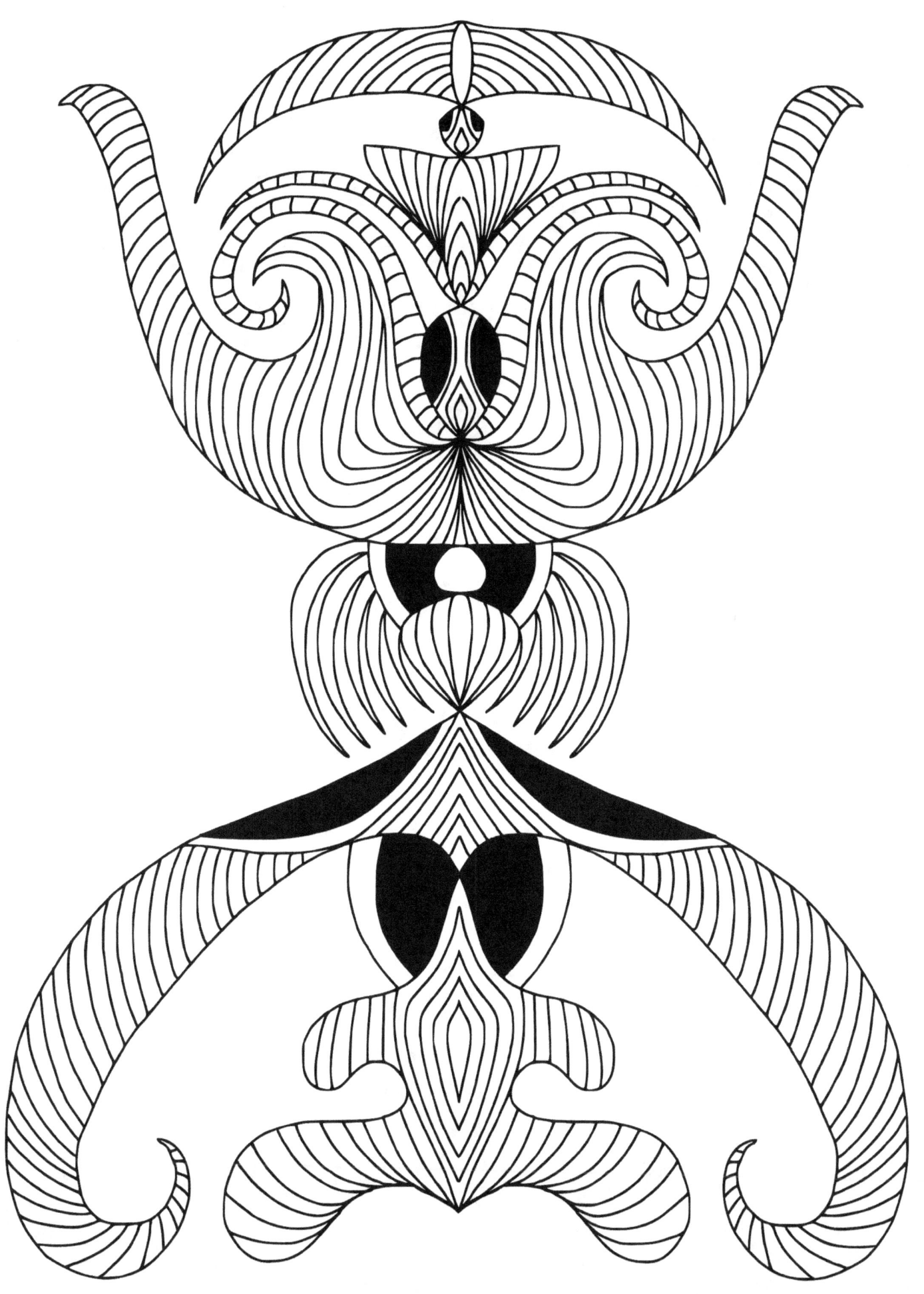

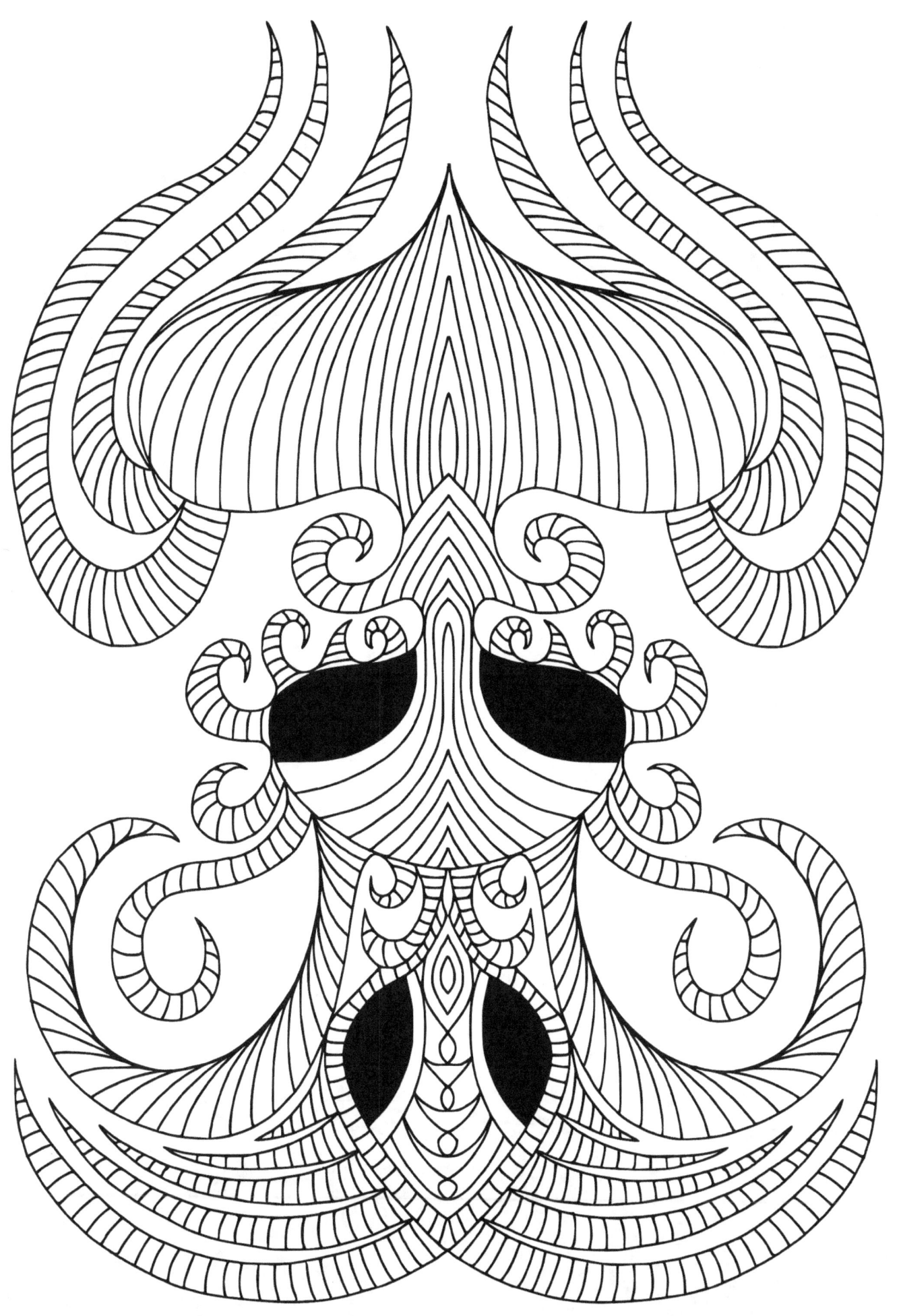

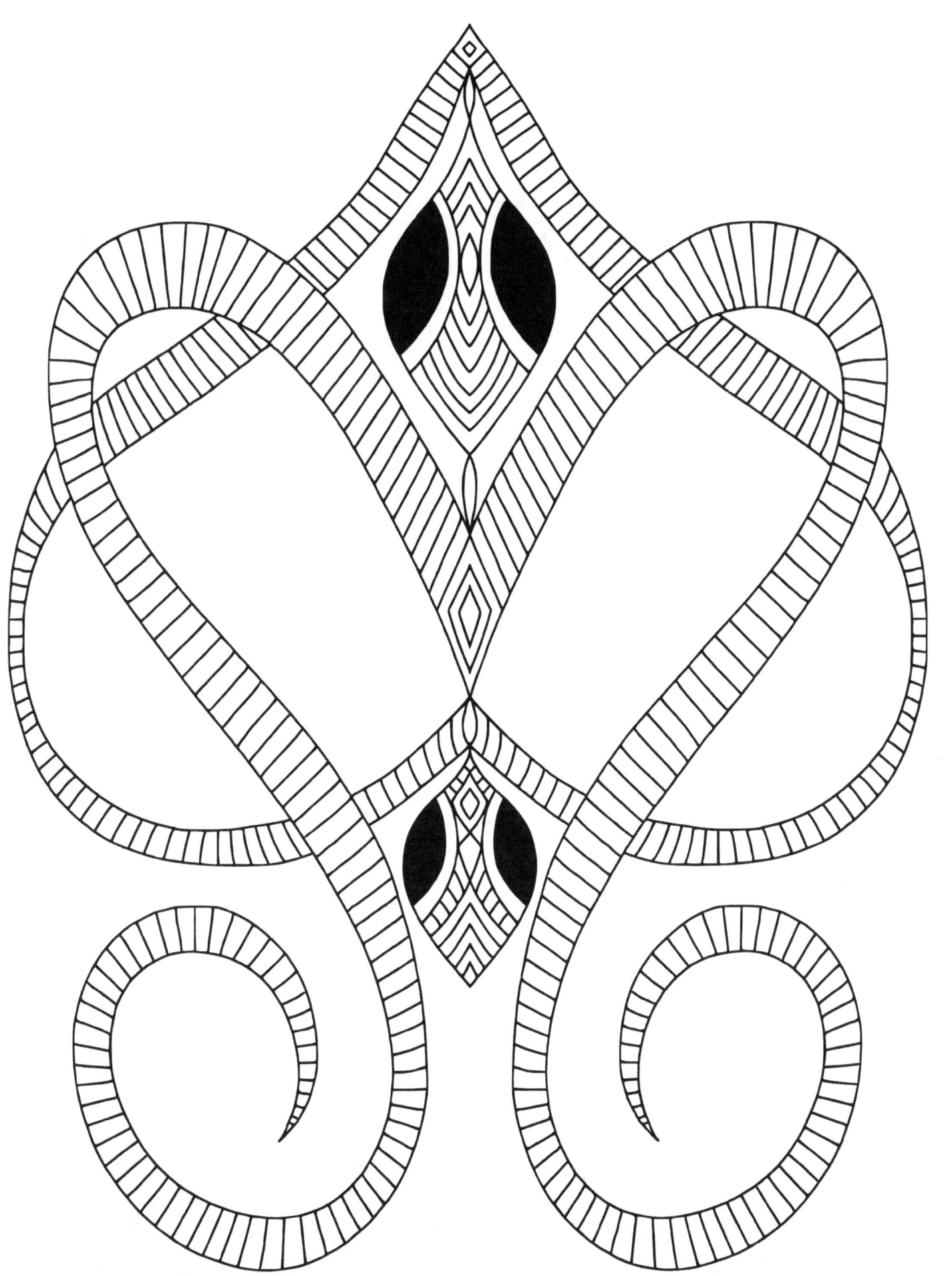

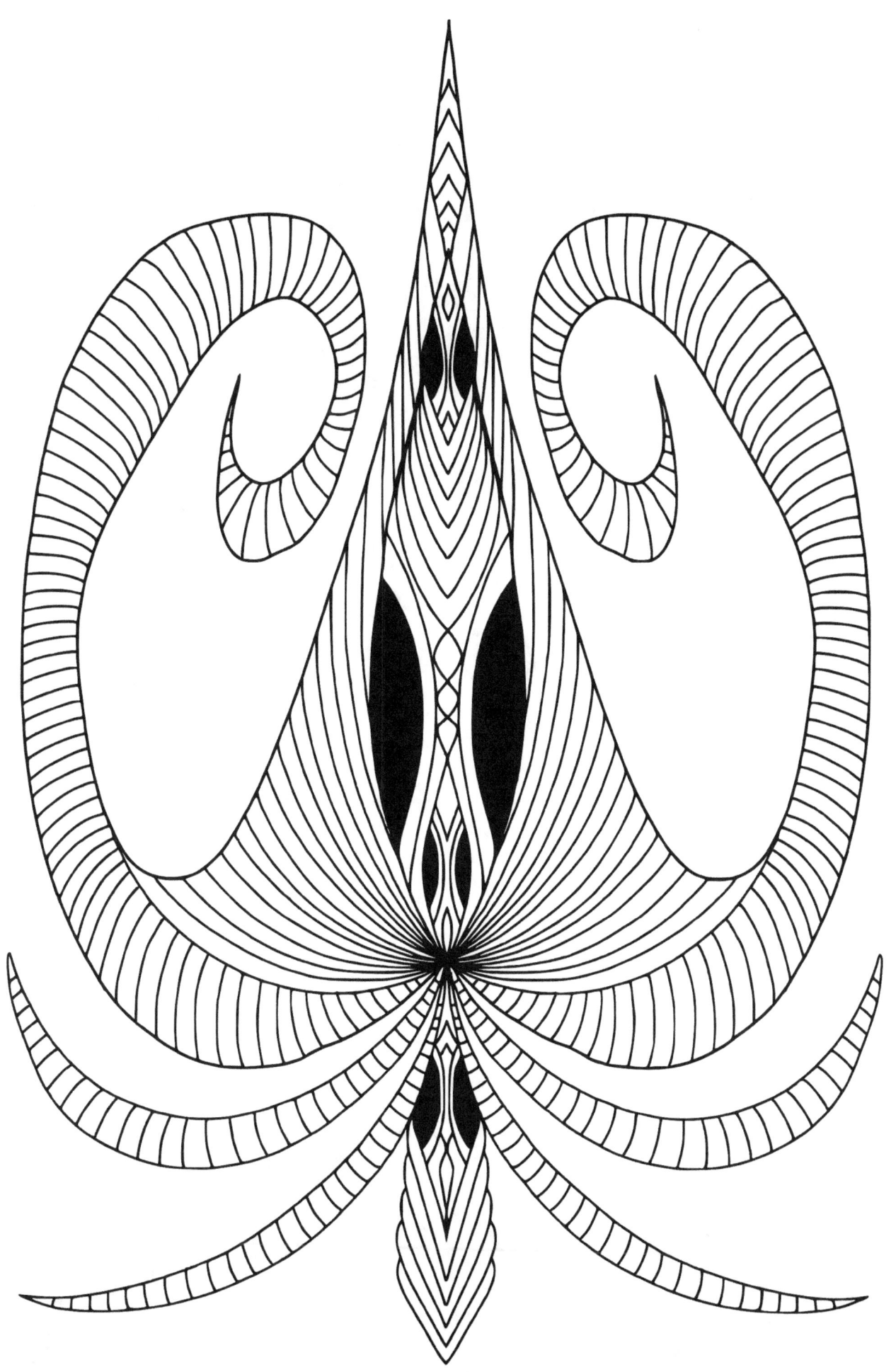

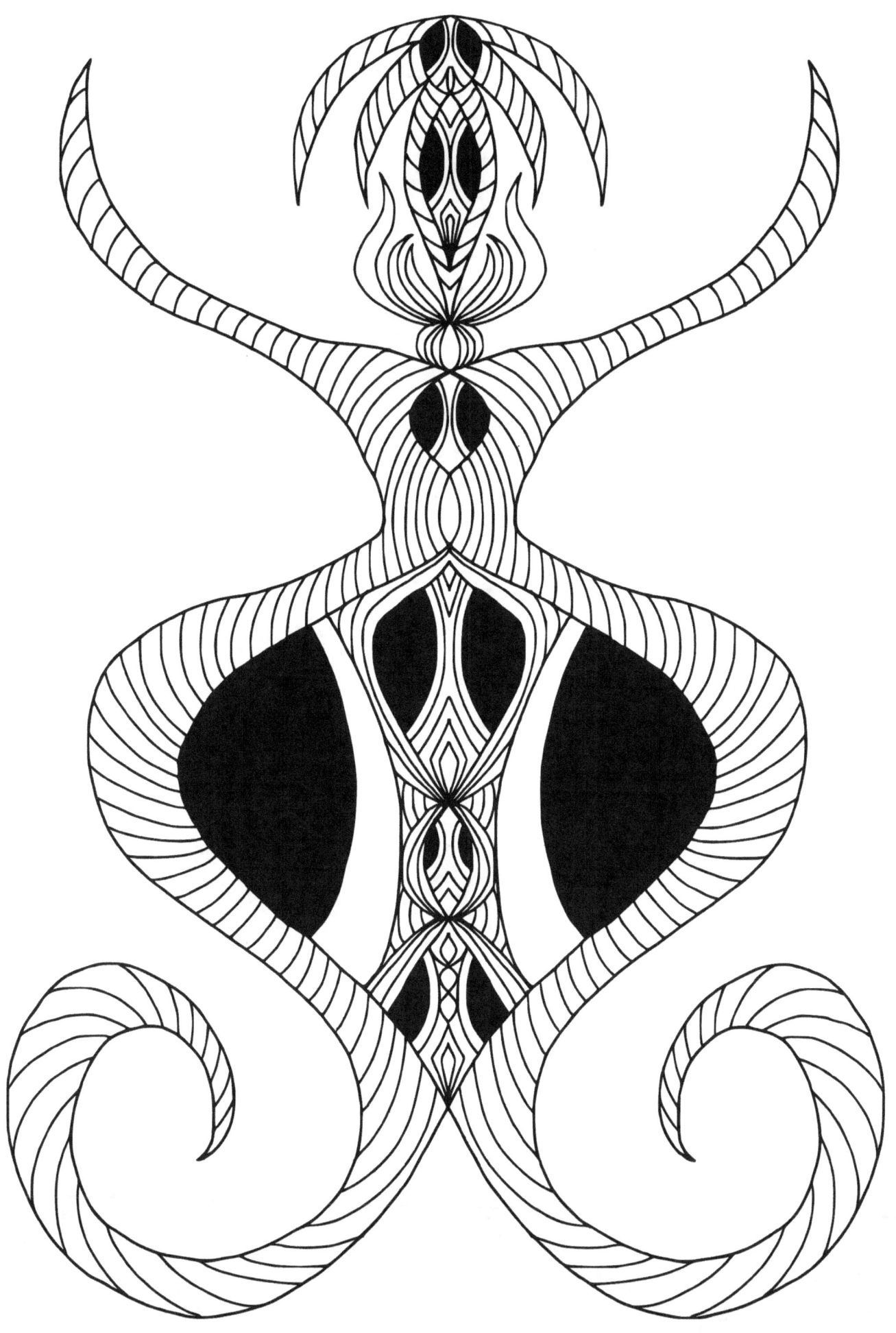

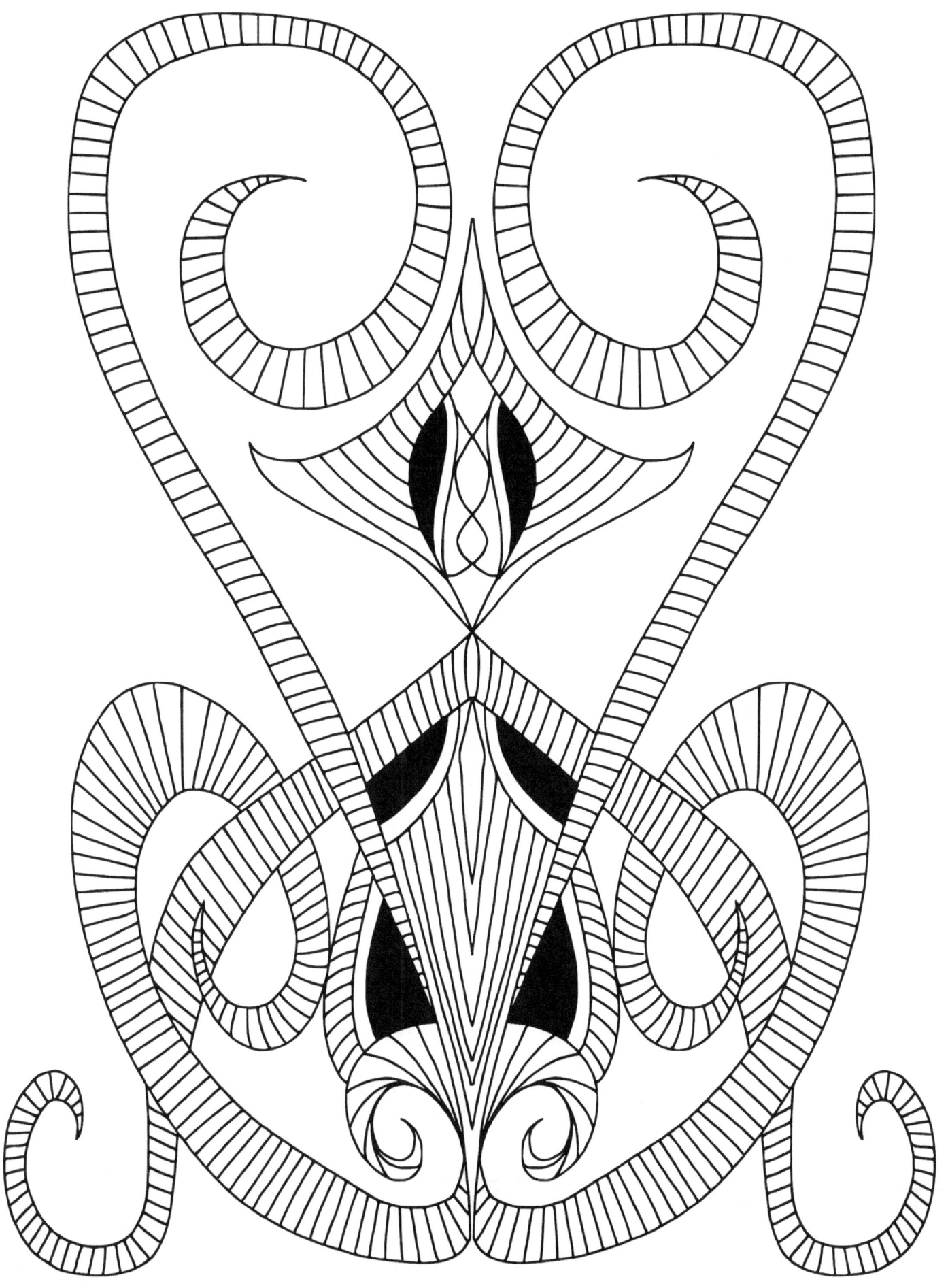

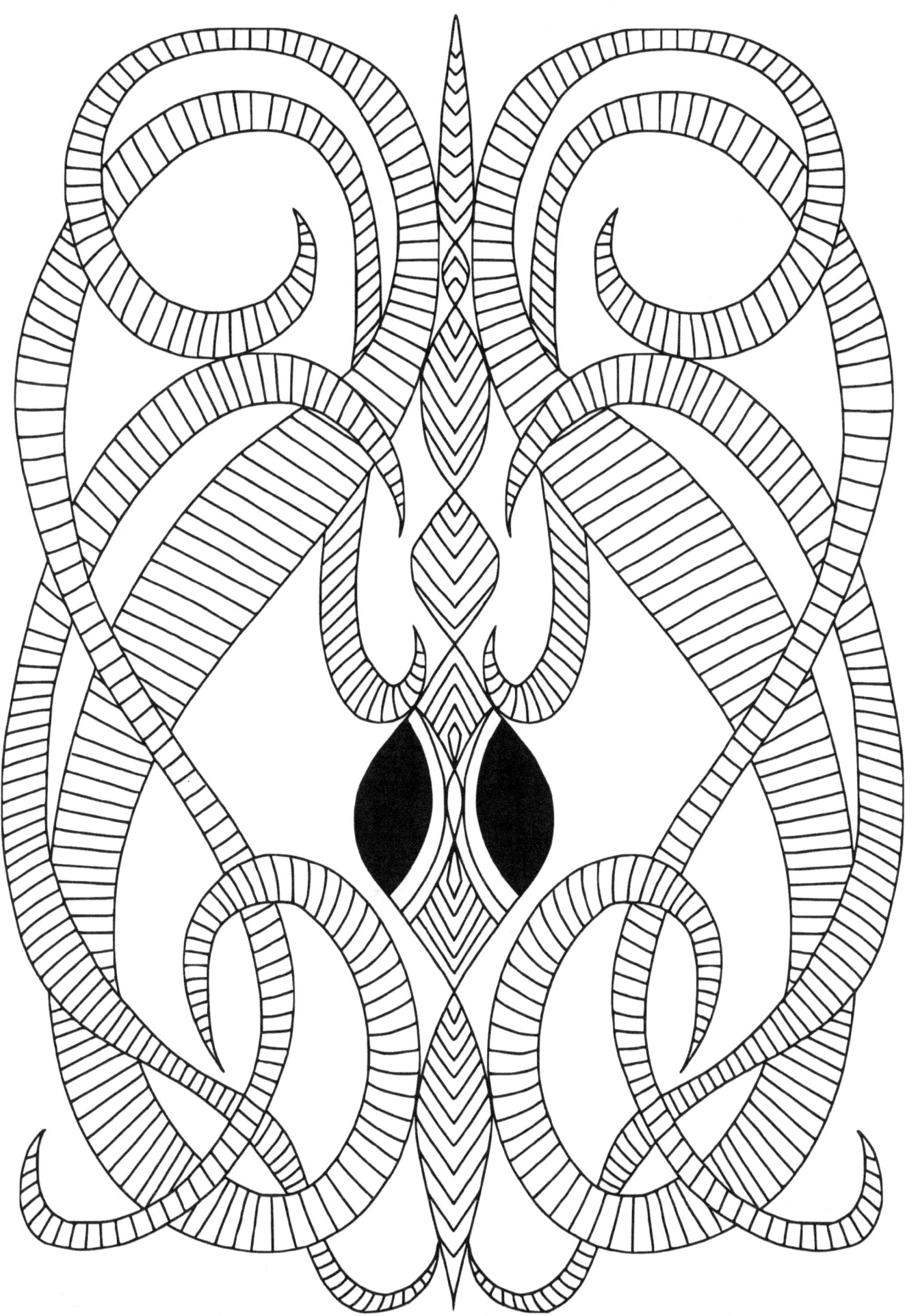

Test your colors here on the samples from
"My Pocket Coloring Companion"
&
"My Coloring Companion"

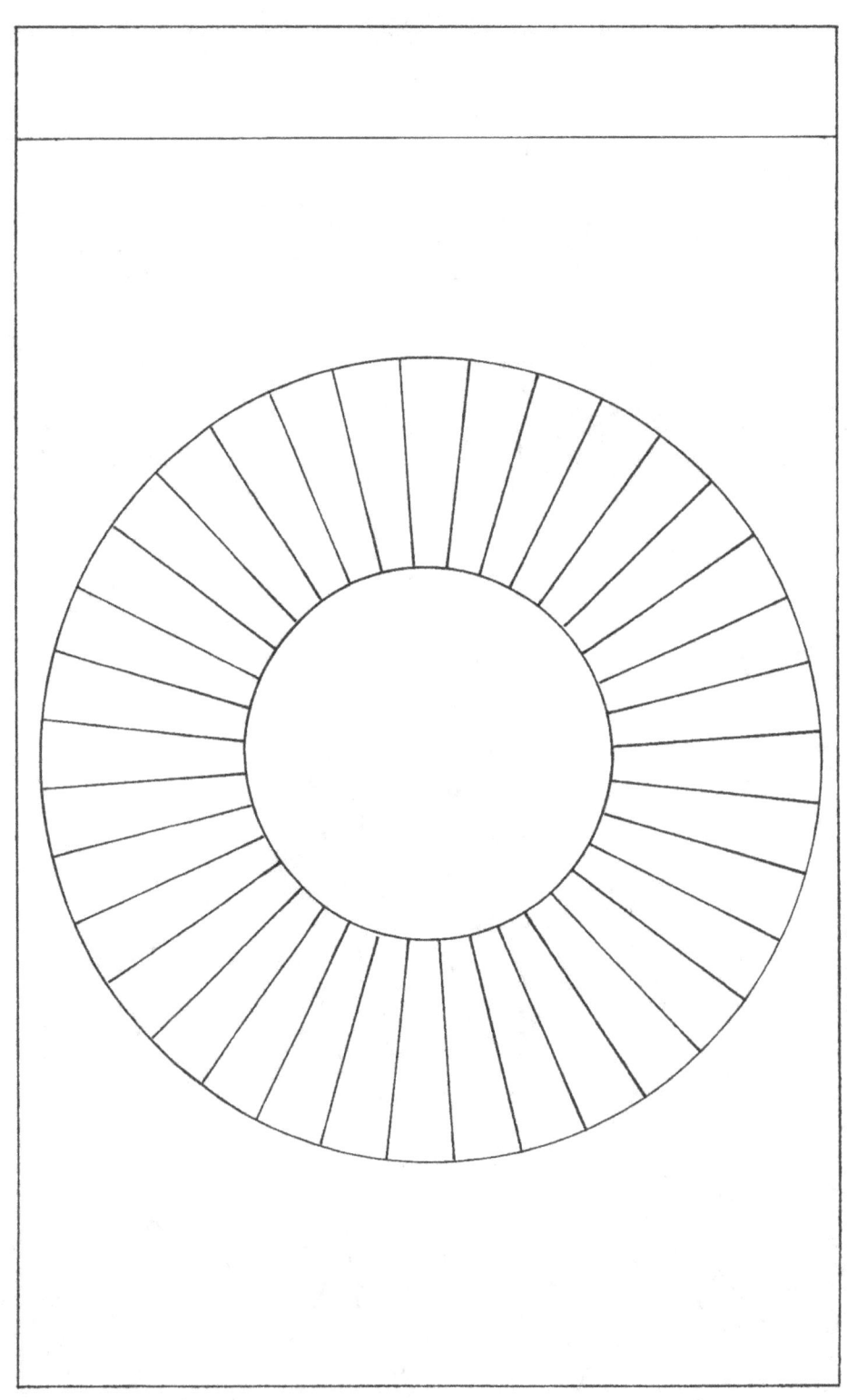

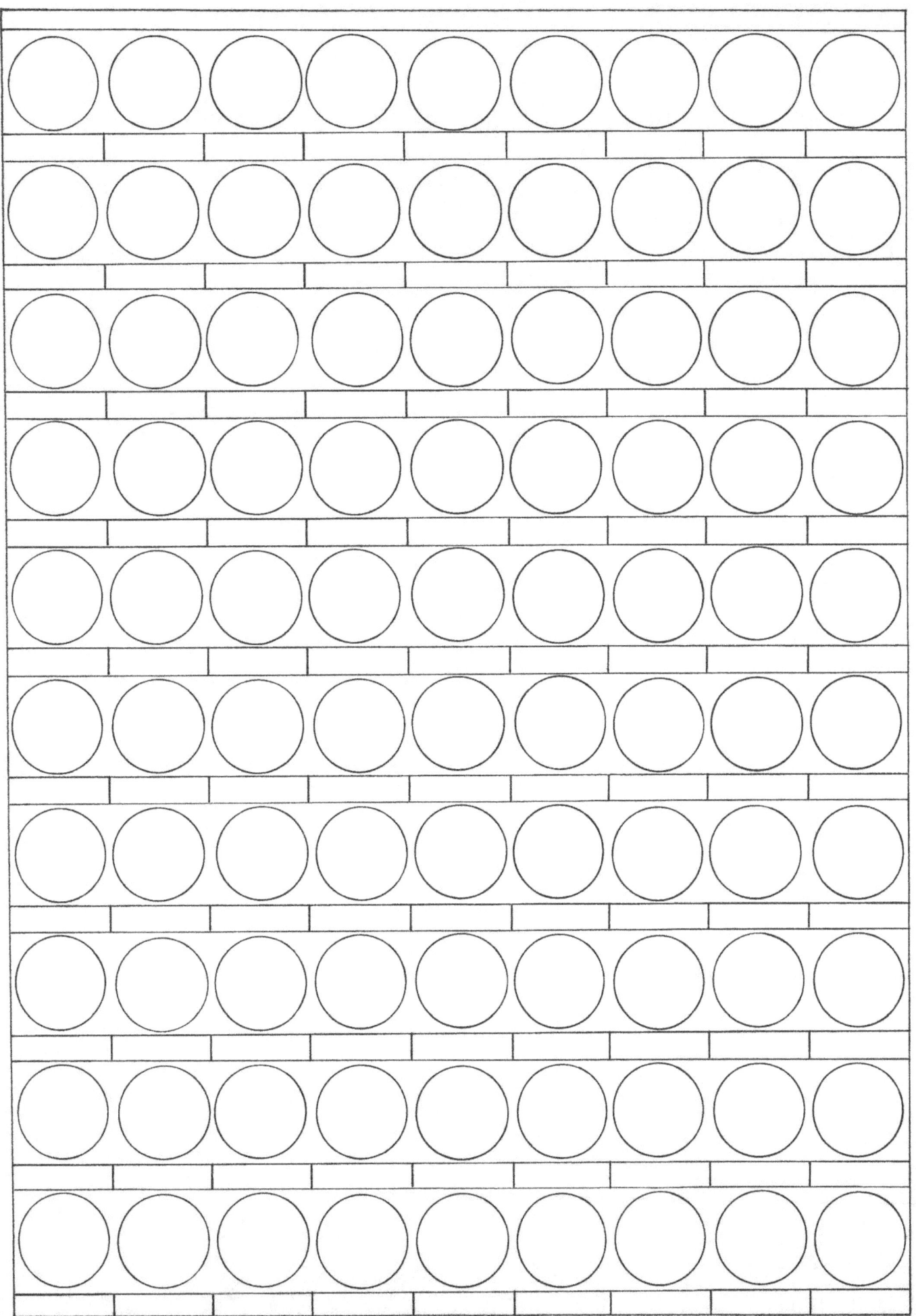